TEACHER'S PET PUBLICATIONS

LITPLAN TEACHER PACK
for
A Farewell to Arms
based on the book by
Ernest Hemingway

Written by
Mary B. Collins and Barbara M. Linde

© 2005 Teacher's Pet Publications
All Rights Reserved

The Lit Plan for *A Farewell to Arms* has been brought to you by Teacher's Pet Publications, Inc.

Copyright Teacher's Pet Publications 2006
All Rights Reserved

Only the student materials in this unit plan may be reproduced. Pages such as worksheets and study guides may be reproduced for use in the purchaser's classroom.

For any additional copyright questions, contact Teacher's Pet Publications.

www.tpet.com

TABLE OF CONTENTS *A Farewell to Arms*

Introduction	7
Unit Objectives	10
Reading Assignment Sheet	11
Unit Outline	12
Study Questions (Short Answer)	15
Quiz/Study Questions (Multiple Choice)	25
Pre-Reading Vocabulary Worksheets	43
Lesson One (Introductory Lesson)	61
Nonfiction Assignment Sheet	68
Oral Reading Evaluation Form	70
Writing Assignment 1	72
Writing Evaluation Form	73
Writing Assignment 2	79
Extra Writing Assignments/ Discussion Questions	85
Quotations	87
Writing Assignment 3	93
Vocabulary Review Activities	94
Unit Review Activities	95
Unit Test	101
Unit Resource Materials	135
Vocabulary Resource Materials	155

A FEW NOTES ABOUT THE AUTHOR
ERNEST HEMINGWAY

HEMINGWAY, Ernest (1899-1961). A writer famous for his terse, direct style, Ernest Hemingway was also known for the way in which his own life mirrored the activities and interests of his characters. Many of his works show man pitted against nature, as in his favorite sports-hunting, fishing, and bullfighting. In others he tells of the experiences of wartime-man against man. The immediate appeal of his best writing probably stems from the fact that he wrote of things he knew intimately and that were important to him.

Ernest Hemingway was born on July 21, 1899, in Oak Park, Ill., a Chicago suburb. His father was a doctor. After high school Hemingway got a job as a reporter on the Kansas City Star. During World War I he tried to enlist in the armed forces but was rejected because of an old eye injury. He volunteered as an ambulance driver on the Italian front, and in 1918 he was badly wounded.

After the war he settled in Paris, France, where he began to write fiction. He submitted his work for criticism to the poet Ezra Pound and to Gertrude Stein, a writer who served as friend and adviser to many writers of the time. The first of many collections of stories, 'In Our Time', published in 1925, did not sell well. His novel 'The Sun Also Rises', which came out a year later, made his name known. It tells of young people in postwar Paris and their search for values in a world that in many ways has lost its meaning.

In 'A Farewell to Arms' (1929), about war on the Italian front, Hemingway tells a love story that is interspersed with scenes of magnificent battle reporting. 'To Have and Have Not' (1937) shows Hemingway's interest in social problems, an interest more fully realized in 'For Whom the Bell Tolls' (1940), set in the Spanish Civil War. In 'Across the River and into the Trees' (1950) an army officer dies while on leave. This novel is generally considered inferior to 'The Old Man and the Sea' (1952), which won a Pulitzer prize in 1953. Hemingway received the Nobel prize for literature in 1954.

Hemingway was a war correspondent in Spain, China, and Europe during World War II. He was married four times and had three sons. Toward the end of his life he suffered from anxiety and depression. He died on July 2, 1961, in his home in Ketchum, Idaho, of a self-inflicted shotgun wound.

--- Courtesy of Compton's Learning Company

INTRODUCTION *A Farewell to Arms*

This unit has been designed to develop students' reading, writing, thinking, listening, and speaking skills through exercises and activities related to *A Farewell to Arms* by Ernest Hemingway It includes 20 lessons, supported by extra resource materials.

The **introductory lesson** introduces students to *A Farewell to Arms* and Hemingway through a video. Following the introductory activity, students are given an explanation of how the activity relates to the book they are about to read. Following the transition, students are given the materials they will be using during the unit. They are also introduced to the nonfiction assignment. At the end of the lesson, students begin the prereading work for the first reading assignment.

The **reading assignments** are approximately 30 pages each; some are a little shorter while others are a little longer. Students have approximately 15 minutes of pre-reading work to do prior to each reading assignment. This pre-reading work involves reviewing the study questions for the assignment and doing some vocabulary work for 8 to 10 vocabulary words they will encounter in their reading.

The **study guide questions** are fact-based questions; students can find the answers to these questions right in the text. These questions come in two formats: short answer or multiple choice. The best use of these materials is probably to use the short answer version of the questions as study guides for students (since answers will be more complete), and to use the multiple-choice version for occasional quizzes. It might be a good idea to make transparencies of your answer keys for the overhead projector.

The **vocabulary work** is intended to enrich students' vocabularies as well as to aid in the students' understanding of the book. Prior to each reading assignment, students will complete a two-part worksheet for approximately 8 to 10 vocabulary words in the upcoming reading assignment. Part I focuses on students' use of general knowledge and contextual clues by giving the sentence in which the word appears in the text. Students are then to write down what they think the words mean based on the words' usage. Part II gives students dictionary definitions of the words and has them match the words to the correct definitions based on the words' contextual usage. Students should then have an understanding of the words when they meet them in the text.

After each reading assignment, students will go back and formulate answers for the study guide questions. Discussion of these questions serves as a review of the most important events and ideas presented in the reading assignments.

After students complete extra discussion questions, there is a vocabulary review lesson which pulls together all of the separate vocabulary lists for the reading assignments and gives students a review of all of the words they have studied.

Following the reading of the book, a lesson is devoted to the extra discussion questions/writing assignments. These questions focus on interpretation, critical analysis and personal response, employing a variety of thinking skills and adding to the students' understanding of the novel. These questions are done as a **group activity**.

Using the information they have acquired so far through individual work and class discussions, students get together to further examine the text and to brainstorm ideas relating to the themes of the novel.

The group activity is followed by a **reports and discussion** session in which the groups share their ideas about the book with the entire class; thus, the entire class gets exposed to many different ideas regarding the themes and events of the book.

There are **three writing assignments** in this unit, each with the purpose of informing, persuading, or having students express personal opinions. The first assignment is to **express personal opinions**. Students will describe war in their own way. The second writing assignment is to **inform**. Students will discuss the point of the novel and how Hemingway uses the characters and events in the novel to convey his message. The third writing assignment is to **persuade**. Students will persuade Frederick Henry to go back to the Italian army.

In addition, there is a **nonfiction reading assignment**. Students are required to read a piece of nonfiction related in some way to *A Farewell to Arms*. After reading their nonfiction pieces, students will fill out a worksheet on which they answer questions regarding facts, interpretation, criticism, and personal opinions. During one class period, students make oral presentations about the nonfiction pieces they have read. This not only exposes all students to a wealth of information; it also gives students the opportunity to practice public speaking.

The **review lesson** pulls together all of the aspects of the unit. The teacher is given four or five choices of activities or games to use which all serve the same basic function of reviewing all of the information presented in the unit.

The **unit test** comes in two formats: all multiple choice matching true/false or with a mixture of matching, short answer, and composition. As a convenience, two different tests for each format have been included.

There are additional **support materials** included with this unit. The **resource materials sections** include suggestions for an in-class library, crossword and word search puzzles related to the novel, and extra vocabulary worksheets. There is a list of **bulletin board ideas** which gives the teacher suggestions for bulletin boards to go along with this unit. In addition, there is a list of extra class activities the teacher could choose from to enhance the unit or as a substitution for an exercise the teacher might feel is inappropriate for his/her class. Answer keys are located directly after the reproducible student materials throughout the unit. Only student materials may be reproduced for use in the purchaser's classroom without violation of copyrights. Contact Teacher's Pet Publications (www.tpet.com) if you have any copyright questions.

UNIT PLAN ADAPTATIONS – *A Farewell to Arms*

Block Schedule

Depending on the length of your class periods, and the frequency with which the class meets, you may wish to choose one of the following options:

- Complete two of the daily lessons in one class period.
- Have students complete all reading and writing activities in class.
- Assign all reading to be completed out of class, and concentrate on the worksheets and discussions in class.
- Assign the projects from the daily lessons at the beginning of the unit, and allow time each day for students to work on them.
- Use some of the Unit and Vocabulary Resource activities during every class.

Gifted & Talented / Advanced Classes

- Emphasize the projects and the extra discussion questions.
- Have students complete all of the writing activities.
- Assign the reading to be completed out of class and focus on the discussions in class.
- Encourage students to develop their own questions.

ESL / ELD

- Assign a partner to help the student read the text aloud.
- Tape record the text and have the student listen and follow along in the text.
- Give the student the study guide worksheets to use as they read.
- Provide pictures and demonstrations to explain difficult vocabulary words and concepts.
- Conduct guided reading lessons, asking students to stop frequently and explain what they have read.
- Show the movie version of the novel and help students identify characters and events, and relate the action in their own words. You may want to show the movie without the sound and explain the actions in your own words.

UNIT OBJECTIVES – *A Farewell to Arms*

1. Through reading *A Farewell to Arms* students will analyze characters and their situations to better understand the themes of the novel.

2. Students will gain a better understanding of Hemingway's "code hero."

3. Students will demonstrate their understanding of the text on four levels: factual, interpretive, critical, and personal.

4. Students will be able to find and define the symbols used in *A Farewell to Arms*.

5. Students will practice reading aloud and silently to improve their skills in each area.

6. Students will enrich their vocabularies and improve their understanding of the novel through the vocabulary lessons prepared for use in conjunction with it.

7. Students will answer questions to demonstrate their knowledge and understanding of the main events and characters in *A Farewell to Arms*.

8. Students will practice writing through a variety of writing assignments.

9. The writing assignments in this are geared to several purposes:
    a. To check the students' reading comprehension
    b. To make students think about the ideas presented by the novel
    c. To make students put those ideas into perspective
    d. To encourage critical and logical thinking
    e. To provide the opportunity to practice good grammar and improve students' use of the English language.

10. Students will read aloud, report, and participate in large and small group discussions to improve their public speaking and personal interaction skills.

READING ASSIGNMENT SHEET
A Farewell To Arms

Date Assigned	Reading Assignment	Complete By This Date
	Book One: Chapters I-VII	
	Book One: Chapters VIII-XII	
	Book Two: Chapters XIII-XVIII	
	Book Two: Chapters XIX-XXIV	
	Book Three: Chapters XXV-XXVII	
	Book Three: Chapters XXVIII-XXXII	
	Book Four: Chapters XXXIII-XXXVII	
	Book Five: Chapters XXXVIII-XLI	

WRITING ASSIGNMENT LOG

Date Assigned	Assignment	Complete By This Date
	Writing Assignment 1	
	Writing Assignment 2	
	Writing Assignment 3	
	Nonfiction Assignment	

UNIT OUTLINE *Farewell to Arms*

1 Introduction	2 PVR Book 1 Ch I-VII	3 Study ?s 1:I-VII PVR 1:VIII-XII Oral Reading Evaluation	4 Study ?s 1:VIII-XII Writing #1	5 PVR 2:XIII-XVIII
6 PVR 2:XIX-XXIV	7 Quiz Book 2 Writing Conf. PVR 3:XXV-XXVII	8 Study?s 3:XXV-XXVII PVR3:XXVIII-XXXII	9 Study?s 3:XXVIII-XXXII Sent. Structure	10 Writing #2
11 PVR 4: XXXIII-XXXVII	12 PVR 5: XXXVIII-XLI	13 Code Hero	14 Extra Discussion Questions	15 Quotations
16 Writing #3	17 Vocabulary Review	18 Unit Review	19 Test	20 Nonfiction Assignment

STUDY GUIDE QUESTIONS

SHORT ANSWER STUDY GUIDE QUESTIONS
A Farewell to Arms

Book One: Chapters I-VII

1. Where and when does the story take place?
2. Who is the narrator? What is his position?
3. Identify Rinaldi. What kind of a man is he?
4. The priest is introduced in the first few chapters. What is his relationship with Frederick Henry? Rinaldi?
5. Rinaldi talks of Miss Barkley as the girl he will marry. How does Frederick Henry get involved with her?
6. Describe Frederick Henry's relationship to Catherine in these first few chapters.
7. What kind of a woman is Catherine Barkley?
8. What is the point of the incident with the soldier who had a rupture in chapter 7?
9. Frederick Henry says, "Well, I knew I would not be killed. Not in this war." What was his reason?
10. Why does Frederick Henry give up the drinking contest?

Book One: Chapters VIII-XII

1. What did Miss Barkley give to Frederick Henry before he left for the attack?
2. While waiting for the attack to begin, Passini said, "There is nothing worse than war." What did Frederick Henry say was worse than war?
3. What did Passini say was the only way to end the war?
4. Under what circumstances was Lt. Henry wounded?
5. Where was Lt. Henry wounded?
6. When Rinaldi comes to visit Frederick Henry at the hospital, he brings cognac and talks about medals for the wounded lieutenant. What is Henry's reaction to talk about medals?
7. What observation did Rinaldi make about himself and Frederick Henry?
8. What did the priest bring to Frederick Henry in the hospital?
9. Describe Frederick Henry's relationship with the priest.
10. Where was Lt. Henry sent after the first hospital?

Short Answer Study Guide Questions *A Farewell to Arms*

Book Two: Chapters XIII-XVIII
  1. Describe Lt. Henry's arrival at the hospital.
  2. Compare/contrast Miss Gage, Mrs. Walker, and Mrs. Van Campen.
  3. Why was Catherine in Milan?
  4. What did Frederick Henry discover about his feelings for Catherine?
  5. Compare and contrast the house doctor (and his two associates) with Dr. Valentini.
  6. Why did Catherine take three nights off of night duty?
  7. Why does Frederick Henry want to marry Catherine? What is her response?

Book Two: Chapters XIX-XXIV
  1. Why doesn't Catherine like Ettore?
  2. Why is Catherine afraid of rain?
  3. Frederick and Catherine bet on Light For Me, a horse they had never heard of. Why?
  4. What is the matter with Catherine?
  5. According to Frederick and Catherine, what is the difference between a coward and a brave person?
  6. Why didn't Frederick go on convalescent leave?
  7. Describe the last evening Frederick Henry and Catherine have before he has to return to duty.
  8. Describe the parting of Frederick and Catherine as he goes away in the carriage.
  9. How does Catherine feel as she and Frederick part?

Book Three: Chapters XXV-XXVII
  1. How has the major changed since Lt. Henry saw him last?
  2. How has Rinaldi changed since Lt. Henry saw him last? How has he stayed the same?
  3. How has the priest changed since Lt. Henry saw him last? How is he the same?
  4. Rinaldi observes that Lt. Henry is acting differently. How does Rinaldi say Lt. Henry is acting?
  5. Frederick Henry says, "I was always embarrassed by the words *sacred, glorious*, and *sacrifice* and the expression *in vain*." Why did he feel that way?
  6. Frederick Henry says that only certain words have dignity. What words are they?
  7. One group was attacking and Lt. Henry said their name was something to be frightened of. What group was he describing?
  8. What work are Lt. Henry, Aymo, Piani, and Bonello doing?

Short Answer Study Guide Questions *A Farewell to Arms*

Book Three: Chapters XXVIII-XXXII
 1. How do Frederick Henry, Bonello, Piani, and Aymo get separated from the rest of their unit?
 2. Why did they leave the main road?
 3. Why did Lt. Henry shoot the sergeant?
 4. What happened to Aymo?
 5. What happened to Bonello?
 6. Why did Frederick Henry jump into the river?
 7. What could his jumping into the river signify symbolically?

Book Four: Chapters XXXIII-XXXVII
 1. Why does Henry want to go to Switzerland?
 2. Where does Frederick Henry meet up with Catherine?
 3. Why do Frederick and Catherine leave the hotel in the middle of the night?
 4. How do Frederick and Catherine escape to Switzerland?
 5. What happened when Frederick and Catherine were arrested in Switzerland?

Book Five: Chapters XXXVIII-XLI
 1. Why doesn't Catherine want to get married once they are situated in Switzerland?
 2. Why did the doctor say beer would be good for Catherine?
 3. What did Catherine and Frederick do in the Swiss mountains?
 4. Why did they move out of the mountains to Lausanne?
 5. What went wrong with Catherine's delivery?
 6. How did Catherine die?

ANSWER KEY: SHORT ANSWER STUDY GUIDE QUESTIONS
A Farewell To Arms

Book One: Chapters I-VII
1. Where and when does the story take place?
    Most of the story takes place in Italy during World War I. (The last book of the story takes place in Switzerland.)

2. Who is the narrator? What is his position?
    Frederick Henry is the narrator. He is an American who has joined up with the Italian ambulance core.

3. Identify Rinaldi. What kind of a man is he?
    Rinaldi is a member of the ambulance core. He enjoys the pleasures of life.

4. The priest is introduced in the first few chapters. What is his relationship with Frederick Henry? Rinaldi?
    He is the object of Rinaldi's teasing and jokes. Frederick Henry doesn't join in the "baiting" of the priest; he gives the priest some respect.

5. Rinaldi talks of Miss Barkley as the girl he will marry. How does Frederick Henry get involved with her?
    Rinaldi is a passionate man, and the objects of his passions change constantly. It doesn't seem to cause him any real stress to "give up" Miss Barkley. He talks to Ferguson, which conveniently gives Frederick and Catherine time to talk with each other. When he sees that Miss Barkley seems to like Henry, he simply takes a "back seat." Perhaps his intent was to introduce them from the start.

6. Describe Frederick Henry's relationship to Catherine in these first few chapters.
    Frederick Henry likes Catherine but is not in love with her and has no intentions of falling in love with her. He likes her but sees their relationship as a game in which one says and does what is expected whether it is meant or not.

7. What kind of a woman is Catherine Barkley?
    Catherine's fiancé was killed in the war. She is a bit vulnerable and "a little crazy" at the time she meets Frederick Henry. She likes him, realizes that their relationship is "a rotten game" and is willing to be involved anyway.

8. What is the point of the incident with the soldier who had a rupture in chapter 7?
    It shows the general negative attitude towards the war.

Answer Key Short Answer Study Guide Questions *A Farewell To Arms*

<u>Book One: Chapters I-VII</u>

9. Frederick Henry says, "Well, I knew I would not be killed. Not in this war." What was his reason?
    "It [the war] did not have anything to do with me."

10. Why does Frederick Henry give up the drinking contest?
    He does not need to win the contest to boost his ego or prove anything, and he remembers he wants to go see Catherine. He is not a sloppy drunk; he remains in control of himself.

<u>Book One: Chapters VIII-XII</u>

1. What did Miss Barkley give to Frederick Henry before he left for the attack?
    She gave him a Saint Anthony medal.

2. While waiting for the attack to begin, Passini said, "There is nothing worse than war." What did Frederick Henry say was worse than war?
    He said that defeat was worse than war.

3. What did Passini say was the only way to end the war?
    He said the only way to end the war was for one side to stop fighting.

4. Under what circumstances was Lt. Henry wounded?
    He was eating macaroni and cheese and drinking wine in a dugout which was hit by a trench mortar shell.

5. Where was Lt. Henry wounded?
    He was wounded in the legs, especially the knees.

6. When Rinaldi comes to visit Frederick Henry at the hospital, he brings cognac and talks about medals for the wounded lieutenant. What is Henry's reaction to talk about medals?
    Lt. Henry sticks to the facts. He doesn't have any interest in finding a way to acquire a medal.

7. What observation did Rinaldi make about himself and Frederick Henry?
    He said they were the same underneath, like brothers.

8. What did the priest bring to Frederick Henry in the hospital?
    He brought vermouth and newspapers.

Answer Key Short Answer Study Guide Questions *A Farewell To Arms*

<u>Book One: Chapters VIII-XII</u>

9. Describe Frederick Henry's relationship with the priest.
　　The priest liked Frederick Henry and Frederick respected the priest. They share good talks and concern for each other.

10. Where was Lt. Henry sent after the first hospital?
　　He was sent to an American hospital in Milan.

<u>Book Two: Chapters XIII-XVIII</u>

1. Describe Lt. Henry's arrival at the hospital.
　　The new hospital was not ready for patients. The nurse on duty seems confused and inept. It is important to note that although he is in pain and the one who is supposed to be being treated, Frederick Henry takes charge. He makes decisions and tells others what to do.

2. Compare/contrast Miss Gage, Mrs. Walker, and Mrs. Van Campen.
　　Mrs. Walker is "too old" and of "no use." Mrs. Van Campen is the supervisor of the hospital. She is "too good for her position" and stern, but we see by her sneaking a little sherry into Frederick's eggnog, that she is not without compassion. Gage is young, intelligent, and compassionate. She will be a friend to Frederick (and Catherine).

3. Why was Catherine in Milan?
　　She was transferred to the new hospital.

4. What did Frederick Henry discover about his feelings for Catherine?
　　He discovered that he had fallen in love with her.

5. Compare and contrast the house doctor (and his two associates) with Dr. Valentini.
　　The three doctors agreed that they should wait to do the operation on Frederick Henry's knee. They would not drink and were presented as "delicate," conferring with one another, each somewhat dependent on the others' opinions. Dr. Valentini is a Hemingway man. He is self-assured, glad to have a drink, makes his own decisions and has the skills to do the job well.

6. Why did Catherine take three nights off of night duty?
　　She took three nights off to try to keep from arousing suspicions about her affair with Frederick Henry.

7. Why does Frederick Henry want to marry Catherine? What is her response?
　　He thinks they should get married. He has concerns about the possibilities of their having a child or his being killed. Also, he doesn't want her to leave him. She considers them already married. "It would mean everything to me if I had any religion. But I haven't any religion."

Answer Key Short Answer Study Guide Questions *A Farewell To Arms*

<u>Book Two: Chapters XIX-XXIV</u>

1. Why doesn't Catherine like Ettore?
    Ettore bores her. He is a war hero who flaunts his medals and rank, things she does not admire.

2. Why is Catherine afraid of rain?
    "I am afraid of the rain because sometimes I see me dead in it."

3. Frederick and Catherine bet on Light For Me, a horse they had never heard of. Why?
    The races were fixed, and Meyers had been giving them tips -- cheating. Catherine didn't want to cheat. Having fun and not cheating were more important than winning money.

4. What is the matter with Catherine?
    She is pregnant.

5. According to Frederick and Catherine, what is the difference between a coward and a brave person?
    "The brave dies perhaps two thousand deaths . . . . He simply doesn't mention them." He keeps his troubles to himself -- and faces them calmly and rationally.

6. Why didn't Frederick go on convalescent leave?
    He got jaundice, his drinking was discovered, and he lost his leave.

7. Describe the last evening Frederick Henry and Catherine have before he has to return to duty.
    They walk and go to a hotel. Catherine momentarily shows unhappiness because she says she "feels like a whore," but soon recovers and is "a good girl again." They share a meal in their hotel room and converse about having a home.

8. Describe the parting of Frederick and Catherine as he goes away in the carriage.
    Frederic says goodbye and gets into the carriage. Catherine smiles and waves to him.

9. How does Catherine feel as she and Frederick part?
    She feels miserable.

Answer Key Short Answer Study Guide Questions *A Farewell To Arms*

Book Three: Chapters XXV-XXVII

1. How has the major changed since Lt. Henry saw him last?
    The major looked older and drier. He said it had been a bad summer, that there were now many sick people. He told Lt. Henry he was tired of the war.

2. How has Rinaldi changed since Lt. Henry saw him last? How has he stayed the same?
    Rinaldi is also tired, worn, and looking older. At dinner, only Rinaldi will "bait" the priest. He wants it to be like the old days, to have others join in, but things and people have changed during the war.

3. How has the priest changed since Lt. Henry saw him last? How is he the same?
    The priest looks the same as before—small, brown, and compact. However, Rinaldi's baiting does not affect him any more.

4. Rinaldi observes that Lt. Henry is acting differently. How does Rinaldi say Lt. Henry is acting?
    Rinaldi says that Lt. Henry is acting like a married man.

5. Frederick Henry says, "I was always embarrassed by the words *sacred, glorious*, and *sacrifice* and the expression in vain." Why did he feel that way?
    Frederick is a man of action, a man who understands and values concrete reality. Abstract words don't mean anything; the actions which cause the words to be used are important -- the words alone are not.

6. Frederick Henry says that only certain words have dignity. What words are they?
    He says that the names of places, such as towns, rivers, roads, and the numbers of regiments and the dates have dignity.

7. One group was attacking and Lt. Henry said their name was something to be frightened of. What group was he describing?
    He was describing the Germans.

8. What work are Lt. Henry, Aymo, Piani, and Bonello doing?
    They are evacuating the field hospitals and the clearing station at Plava.

Answer Key Short Answer Study Guide Questions *A Farewell To Arms*

Book Three: Chapters XXVIII-XXXIII

1. How do Frederick Henry, Bonello, Piani, and Aymo get separated from the rest of their unit?
    They had helped to evacuate the rest of their post for the retreat and were to bring the "junk they've left" to Pordenone after tending to their vehicles. They are so tired they decide to get a little sleep before beginning their trip.

2. Why did they leave the main road?
    They thought the main road would be attacked and that their chances for a successful trip would be better on the side roads.

3. Why did Lt. Henry shoot the sergeant?
    The sergeant would not obey the order to help push the cars out of the mud. The sergeants showed no respect for order or discipline.

4. What happened to Aymo?
    He was shot by mistake by Italians along the railroad bank.

5. What happened to Bonello?
    He left Frederick Henry and Piani at the farmhouse. One could presume he deserted the army since Piani said, "You see we don't believe in the war anyway, Tenente."

6. Why did Frederick Henry jump into the river?
    The battle police were questioning officers and killing them. He feared for his life and escaped into the river.

7. What could his jumping into the river signify symbolically?
    It could signify his farewell to arms, his washing himself of the whole war, which has degenerated into total chaos. There is nothing he values left in the war; he moves on to a new stage in his life.

Answer Key Short Answer Study Guide Questions *A Farewell To Arms*

Book Four: Chapters XXXIII-XXXVII
1. Why does Henry want to go to Switzerland?
    Switzerland is a neutral country. He can get away from those who are looking for him.

2. Where does Frederick Henry meet up with Catherine?
    He finds her at Stresa.

3. Why do Frederick and Catherine leave the hotel in the middle of the night?
    The barman comes in to warn Frederick that he will be arrested in the morning.

4. How do Frederick and Catherine escape to Switzerland?
    The barman gives them a boat and food.

5. What happened when Frederick and Catherine were arrested in Switzerland?
    Their passports were checked, and they were questioned. They told the police that they wanted winter sport. The police believed them and freed them to go to the town of their choice.

Book Five: Chapters XXXVIII-XLI
1. Why doesn't Catherine want to get married once they are situated in Switzerland?
    "It's too embarrassing now. I show too plainly."

2. Why did the doctor say beer would be good for Catherine?
    It would keep the baby small. This is the first hint of possible trouble with Catherine's pregnancy.

3. What did Catherine and Frederick do in the Swiss mountains?
    They played, walked, talked, and ate. It was a lazy, happy time for them.

4. Why did they move out of the mountains to Lausanne?
    They wanted to be closer to the hospital. Also, the bad, rainy weather had come to the mountains.

5. What went wrong with Catherine's delivery?
    The baby wouldn't come; she had to have a Caesarean delivery. The baby was choked by the cord and born dead.

6. How did Catherine die?
    She had hemorrhages after the Caesarean operation.

MULTIPLE CHOICE STUDY GUIDE/QUIZ QUESTIONS *A Farewell to Arms*

<u>Book One: Chapters I-VII</u>
1. Where and when does the story take place?
    A. in Austria during World War II
    B. in Italy during World War I
    C. in Germany during World War I
    D. in France during World War II

2. Who is the narrator?
    A. Frederick Henry
    B. Ernest Hemingway
    C. the narrator is not named
    D. Aldo Bertolli

3. The narrator is _____.
    A. Italian
    B. American
    C. German
    D. French

4. Which statement describes Rinaldi?
    A. He is a general in the Italian army and is quite unpleasant.
    B. He is a mechanic who repairs the Italian tanks and has many friends.
    C. He is a surgeon in the ambulance corps who enjoys the pleasures of life.
    D. He is a villager who does not like soldiers.

5. Which statement describes the priest's relationship with Rinaldi and Frederick Henry?
    A. They both respect the priest.
    B. Rinaldi reveres him but Henry ignores him.
    C. Rinaldi dislikes him but Henry thinks he is kind and gentle.
    D. Rinaldi teases him but Henry gives him some respect.

6. Rinaldi says he wants to _____.
    A. move to America after the war is over
    B. start his own medical practice
    C. survive the war without being injured
    D. marry Miss Barkley

7. True or False: In the first few chapters of Book I, Frederick Henry is madly in love with Catherine.
    A. True
    B. False

Multiple Choice Study Guide/Quiz Questions *A Farewell to Arms*

Book One: Chapters I-VII Continued

8. The narrator describes Catherine Barkley as _____.
   A. lovely and highly intelligent
   B. a dark and mysterious beauty
   C. vulnerable and a little crazy
   D. confident and happy

9. In Chapter 7, the incident with the soldier who had a rupture shows _____.
   A. the primitive state of medicine at the time of the war
   B. Henry's compassion for others
   C. the general negative attitude towards the war
   D. the soldier's disregard for authority

10. True or False: Frederick Henry says he would not be killed in the war.
    A. True
    B. False

11. Frederick Henry gives up the _____ so he can see Catherine.
    A. extra pay for working overtime
    B. drinking contest
    C. poker game
    D. night out on the town

Multiple Choice Study Guide/Quiz Questions *A Farewell to Arms*

Book One: Chapters VIII-XII

1. What did Miss Barkley give to Frederick Henry before he left for the attack?
    A. a white lace handkerchief
    B. a letter for him to read in one week
    C. a Saint Anthony medal
    D. a package of cookies

2. While waiting for the attack to begin, Passini said, "There is nothing worse than war." Frederick Henry replied, "_____ is worse."
    A. Defeat
    B. A broken heart
    C. Death
    D. Hatred

3. Passini said that the only way to end a war was _____.
    A. for one side to wipe out the other side
    B. to never start in the first place
    C. for both sides to destroy the other
    D. for one side to stop fighting

4. What were Frederick Henry and the others doing when he was wounded?
    A. They were tending the sick at an army hospital.
    B. They were playing cards.
    C. They were sleeping.
    D. They were eating a meal in the dugout.

5. Where was Lt. Henry wounded?
    A. He was wounded in the legs, especially the knees.
    B. He was wounded in the arms and hands.
    C. He was wounded in the back.
    D. He was wounded in the chest and neck.

6. When Rinaldi comes to visit Frederick Henry at the hospital, he talks about medals for the wounded lieutenant. What is Henry's reaction to the talk about medals?
    A. He agrees and makes up a story about his injuries.
    B. He doesn't have any interest in finding a way to get a medal.
    C. He says he deserves a silver medal.
    D. He says the others who were with him should get medals, too.

Multiple Choice Study Guide/Quiz Questions *A Farewell to Arms*

Book One: Chapters VIII-XII Continued

7. What observation did Rinaldi make about himself and Frederick Henry?
    A. He said they were the same underneath, like brothers.
    B. He said they would always be strangers to each other.
    C. He said they both liked to love beautiful women.
    D. He said they would never understand each other.

8. What did the priest bring to Frederick Henry in the hospital?
    A. a Bible and a letter from Catherine
    B. wine and cheese
    C. Holy Communion and a rosary
    D. vermouth and newspapers

9. True or False: The priest liked Frederick Henry and Frederick Henry respected the priest.
    A. True
    B. False

10. Lt. Henry was sent to _____.
    A. an Italian hospital in Sicily
    B. an allied hospital in Germany
    C. an American hospital in Milan
    D. an army hospital in the United States

Multiple Choice Study Guide/Quiz Questions *A Farewell to Arms*

Book Two: Chapters XIII-XVIII

1. True or False: The new hospital where Frederick Henry went was all ready for patients when he arrived.
    A. True
    B. False

2. Mrs. Walker was _____.
    A. highly efficient
    B. secretly in love with Frederick Henry
    C. too old and of no use
    D. slow but helpful

3. Mrs. Van Campen was _____.
    A. stern and too good for her position
    B. the best nurse in Italy
    C. mean to the patients
    D. kind and compassionate

4. Which word does not describe Miss Gage?
    A. compassionate
    B. young
    C. intelligent
    D. unattractive

5. Why was Catherine Barkley in Milan?
    A. She was recovering from a nervous breakdown.
    B. She was transferred to the new hospital.
    C. She was on leave.
    D. She was getting supplies for the soldiers.

6. What did Frederick Henry discover about his feelings for Catherine?
    A. He was in love with her.
    B. His feelings had not changed.
    C. He did not like her as much.
    D. Nothing. He did not think about his feelings.

7. Which doctor said that he would operate on Frederick Henry's knee the following day?
    A. Dr. Valentini
    B. Dr. Maggiore
    C. Dr. Varella
    D. Greco

Multiple Choice Study Guide/Quiz Questions *A Farewell to Arms*

Book Two: Chapters XIII-XVIII

8. What did Catherine do to help keep from arousing suspicions about her affair with Frederick Henry?
    A. She stopped talking to Frederick.
    B. She started dating one of the doctors.
    C. She took three nights off of night duty.
    D. She made up a story about a boyfriend who was away at the war.

9. True or False: Frederick Henry wants to marry Catherine Barkley.
    A. True
    B. False

10. Catherine tells Frederick that he is her _____.
    A. only way to escape from the war
    B. religion
    C. distraction from boredom
    D. soul mate

Multiple Choice Study Guide/Quiz Questions *A Farewell to Arms*

Book Two: Chapters XIX-XXIV

1. Why doesn't Catherine like Ettore?
    A. He bores her. She does not admire his medals and rank, which he flaunts.
    B. He made a pass at her.
    C. He insulted the nursing profession.
    D. She does not trust him, and thinks he may be a spy.

2. Catherine sometimes sees herself dead in the _____.
    A. snow
    B. hot sun
    C. rain
    D. extreme cold

3. Frederick and Catherine went to the races, which were fixed. Did they take advantage of the tips they got and bet on the horse that was suggested to them?
    A. Yes
    B. No

4. What is the matter with Catherine?
    A. She is depressed.
    B. She is schizophrenic.
    C. She has cancer.
    D. She is pregnant.

5. According to Catherine and Frederick, "The _____ dies perhaps two thousand deaths… he simply doesn't mention them."
    A. brave
    B. soldier
    C. coward
    D. martyr

6. Why didn't Frederick go on convalescent leave?
    A. He had jaundice and his drinking was discovered.
    B. He was not able to walk.
    C. He did not have enough money.
    D. He was afraid to leave the hospital.

Multiple Choice Study Guide/Quiz Questions *A Farewell to Arms*

Book Two: Chapters XIX-XXIV Continued

7. What do Frederick and Catherine do on their last evening before he has to return to duty?
    A. They shop for wedding rings.
    B. They share a meal in their hotel room and talk about having a home.
    C. Nothing. They are not able to be together.
    D. They take a long walk along the river.

8. What does Catherine do when she and Frederick part?
    A. She cries.
    B. She turns and looks the other way.
    C. She hangs onto the handle of the car door.
    D. She smiles and waves.

9. How does Catherine feel as she and Frederick part?
    A. happy
    B. angry
    C. miserable
    D. serene

Multiple Choice Study Guide/Quiz Questions *A Farewell to Arms*

Book Three: Chapters XXV-XXVII

1. True or False: The major looks older and drier since Lt. Henry saw him last.
    A. True
    B. False

2. How has Rinaldi changed since Lt. Henry saw him last?
    A. Rinaldi has lost weight and looks years younger.
    B. Rinaldi has become bitter and sarcastic.
    C. Rinaldi is tired, worn, and looking older.
    D. Rinaldi has become very religious.

3. How has the priest changed since Lt. Henry saw him last?
    A. He is beginning to have doubts in a God who would allow wars.
    B. He has gone bald and is even shorter.
    C. He has become less tolerant of men who are not Catholic.
    D. He is no longer affected by Rinaldi's baiting.

4. Rinaldi observes that Lt. Henry is acting differently. How does Rinaldi say Lt. Henry is acting?
    A. Rinaldi says that Lt. Henry is acting like a married man.
    B. Rinaldi says that Lt. Henry is acting like a cripple.
    C. Rinaldi says that Lt. Henry is acting even more Italian than before.
    D. Rinaldi says that Lt. Henry is behaving like a spoiled officer.

5. Frederick Henry says, "I was always embarrassed by the words _____ because he thinks the actions that cause the words to be used are important, not the words.
    A. love, marriage, family, and fidelity
    B. heroic, brave, loyal, and friendship
    C. sacred, glorious, sacrifice, and in vain
    D. battle, defeat, defense, and underground opposition

6. Frederick Henry says that only certain words have dignity. What words are they?
    A. The words are the names of places, such as towns, rivers, roads, and the numbers of regiments and the dates.
    B. The words are the names of people who are dear to him.
    C. The words are fight, win, conquer, overcome, and victory.
    D. Only words that have to do with peace and prosperity have dignity.

Multiple Choice Study Guide/Quiz Questions *A Farewell to Arms*

Book Three: Chapters XXV-XXVII Continued

7. One group was attacking, and Lt. Henry said their name was something to be frightened of. What group was he describing?
	A. He was describing the Americans.
	B. He was describing the French.
	C. He was describing the Germans.
	D. He was describing the Swiss.

8. What work are Lt. Henry, Aymo, Piani, and Bonello doing?
	A. They are training nurses in Udine.
	B. They are fixing cars in Gorizia.
	C. They are taking care of orphans in Cividale.
	D. They are evacuating the field hospitals and the clearing station at Plava.

Multiple Choice Study Guide/Quiz Questions *A Farewell to Arms*

Book Three Chapters XXVIII-XXXII

1. How did Frederick Henry, Bonello, Piani, and Aymo get separated from the rest of their unit?
    A. They were tired and fell asleep.
    B. They got lost in the dark.
    C. Aymo said he knew a short cut, but it was actually a longer route.
    D. They stopped to wash in a stream and fell behind.

2. Why did they leave the main road?
    A. The main road was blocked by a mudslide.
    B. Their commander told them to take another route.
    C. They thought they would have a more successful trip on the side road.
    D. The main road had been bombed.

3. Why did Lt. Henry shoot the sergeant?
    A. He thought the sergeant was an enemy soldier.
    B. The sergeant did not show respect for order or discipline. He refused to help push the cars out of the mud.
    C. It looked like the sergeant was going to shoot him, so Lt. Henry shot first.
    D. The sergeant insulted Catherine and Lt. Henry got angry.

4. What happened to Aymo?
    A. He got food poisoning from spoiled rations and died.
    B. He was captured by the enemy.
    C. He was released from service because his mother died.
    D. He was shot by mistake by Italians along the railroad bank.

5. What happened to Bonello?
    A. He left Frederick and Piani at the farmhouse.
    B. He was attacked by a pack of mad dogs and died.
    C. He went on leave and did not come back.
    D. He was promoted and transferred to another unit.

Multiple Choice Study Guide/Quiz Questions *A Farewell to Arms*

Book Three Chapters XXVIII-XXXII Continued

6. Frederick Henry jumped into the river because he was afraid _____ would kill him.
    A. the advancing Austrian army
    B. the loneliness of being without Catherine
    C. the Italian battle police
    D. the infection in his legs

7. What could Henry's jumping into the river signify symbolically?
    A. His farewell to arms, washing himself of the war.
    B. His desire to return to the religion of his childhood.
    C. His wish to rid himself of the restrictions of love.
    D. His desire to go back to America.

Multiple Choice Study Guide/Quiz Questions *A Farewell to Arms*

Book Four: Chapters XXXIII-XXXVII

1. Henry wants to go to Switzerland because _____.
    A. the best pediatricians are there
    B. it is a neutral country
    C. he needs another knee surgery
    D. he has a bank account there

2. Where does Frederick meet up with Catherine?
    A. in Berlin
    B. in Stockholm
    C. in Paris
    D. in Stresa

3. Why do Frederick and Catherine leave the hotel in the middle of the night?
    A. They are hungry and want a late dinner.
    B. They decide to get married.
    C. They get a warning that he will be arrested in the morning.
    D. They need medicine because Catherine has a fever.

4. Who gives them the boat and food?
    A. the barman
    B. a nurse friend of Catherine's
    C. the owner of the hotel
    D. the village priest

5. What did Frederick and Catherine tell the police when they were arrested in Switzerland?
    A. They said they were on their honeymoon.
    B. They told the police they wanted winter sport.
    C. They said they were moving to Switzerland for the good of their baby.
    D. They said they were lost and thought they were in Italy.

6. Did the police believe them?
    A. Yes
    B. No

Multiple Choice Study Guide/Quiz Questions *A Farewell to Arms*

Book Five: Chapters XXXVIII-XLI

1. Why doesn't Catherine want to get married once they are situated in Switzerland?
    A. She does not believe in marriage at all.
    B. She is embarrassed because her pregnancy shows too plainly.
    C. She wants to be married in the United States.
    D. She thinks it is frivolous to get married during wartime.

2. Why did the doctor say that beer would be good for Catherine?
    A. It would help her to sleep.
    B. It would fill her up when she was hungry.
    C. It would keep the baby small.
    D. It would calm her nerves.

3. What did Catherine and Frederick do in the Swiss mountains?
    A. They played, walked, talked, and ate.
    B. Frederick skied and Catherine watched him.
    C. They made wedding plans.
    D. They read and wrote letters.

4. Why did they move out of the mountains to Lausanne?
    A. There was more to do in Lausanne.
    B. They were too cold in the mountains.
    C. It was cheaper to live in Lausanne.
    D. They wanted to be closer to the hospital.

5. True or False: The delivery of the baby goes well and a healthy girl is born.
    A. True
    B. False

6. How did Catherine die?
    A. She had hemorrhages after the Caesarean operation.
    B. She got blood poisoning from a transfusion.
    C. She got pneumonia.
    D. She had a heart attack.

ANSWER KEY MULTIPLE CHOICE STUDY/QUIZ QUESTIONS
A Farewell To Arms

	Book 1 I-VII	Book 1 VIII-XII	Book 2 XIII-XVIII	Book 2 XIX-XXIV	Book 3 XXV-XXVII	Book 3 XXVIII-XXXII
1	B	C	B	A	A	A
2	A	A	C	C	C	C
3	B	D	A	B	D	B
4	C	D	D	D	A	D
5	D	A	B	A	C	A
6	D	B	A	A	A	C
7	B	A	A	B	C	A
8	C	D	C	D	D	
9	C	A	A	C		
10	A	C	B			
11	B					

	Book 4 XXXIII-XXXVII	Book 5 XXXVIII-XLI
1	B	B
2	D	C
3	C	A
4	A	D
5	B	B
6	A	A

PREREADING VOCABULARY WORKSHEETS

Prereading Vocabulary Worksheets *A Farewell to Arms*

Book One: Chapters I-VII
Part I: Using Prior Knowledge and Contextual Clues
Below are the sentences in which the vocabulary words appear in the text. Read the sentence. Use any clues you can find in the sentence combined with your prior knowledge, and write what you think the underlined word means in the space provided.

1. There was fighting in the mountains and at night we could see the flashes from the artillery.
_____

2. At the start of the winter came the permanent rain and with the rain came the cholera.
_____

3. "All thinking men are atheists," the major said.
_____

4. "Don't bring Caruso. He bellows."
_____

5. When I came back to the front we still lived in that town.
_____

6. The battery in the next garden woke me in the morning and I saw the sun coming through the window and got out of the bed.
_____

7. "It's a silly front," she said. "But it's very beautiful. Are they going to have an offensive?"
_____

8. "It's not my leg. I got a rupture.
_____

9. "They won't let me. The lieutenant said I slipped the truss on purpose."
_____

10. "Listen, lieutenant. Do you have to take me to that regiment?"
_____

41

Prereading Vocabulary Worksheets *A Farewell to Arms*
Book One: Chapters I-VII Continued

Part II: Determining the Meaning: Match the vocabulary words to their dictionary definitions.

_____ 1. artillery   A. shout in a loud, deep voice

_____ 2. cholera   B. an attack or assault

_____ 3. atheists   C. a disease of the intestines caused by a bacteria

_____ 4. bellows   D. a medical device to support a hernia

_____ 5. front   E. large guns and cannons

_____ 6. battery   F. a grouping of military troops

_____ 7. offensive   G. the leading position in a war

_____ 8. rupture   H. a tear in tissue in the body; a hernia

_____ 9. truss   I. people who do not believe in God or gods

_____ 10. regiment   J. a unit of guns or other weapons

Prereading Vocabulary Worksheets *A Farewell to Arms*

Book One: Chapters VIII-XII
Part I: Using Prior Knowledge and Contextual Clues
Below are the sentences in which the vocabulary words appear in the text. Read the sentence. Use any clues you can find in the sentence combined with your prior knowledge, and write what you think the underlined word means in the space provided.

1. The road went up the valley a long way and then we turned off and commenced to climb the hills again.

   _____

2. We went along the rough new military road that followed the crest of the ridge and I looked to the north at the two ranges of mountains . . .

   _____

3. The ovens and some deep holes had been equipped as dressing stations.

   _____

4. He said that if the thing went well he would see that I was decorated.

   _____

5. "They hang you. They come and make you be a soldier again. Not in the auto-ambulance, in the infantry.

   _____

6. There were big search-lights on that front mounted on camions that you passed sometimes on the roads at night, close behind the lines . . . .

   _____

7. I tried to get closer to Passini to try to put a tourniquet on the legs but I could not move.

   _____

8. He said there was so much dirt blown into the wound that there had not been much hemorrhage.

   _____

Prereading Vocabulary Worksheets *A Farewell to Arms*
Book One: Chapters VIII-XII Continued

9. "Your blood <u>coagulates</u> beautifully.

_____

10. Captain doctor (interested in what he was finding), "<u>Fragments</u> of enemy trench-mortar shell. Now I'll probe for some of this if you like but it's not necessary."

_____

Part II: Determining the Meaning: Match the vocabulary words to their dictionary definitions.

_____ 1. commenced   A. a long, narrow hilltop

_____ 2. ridge   B. buses or trucks

_____ 3. dressing   C. thickens into a soft mass

_____ 4. decorated   D. pertaining to treating wounds

_____ 5. infantry   E. loss of blood

_____ 6. camions   F. given a medal or other honor

_____ 7. tourniquet   G. started

_____ 8. hemorrhage   H. small pieces of something that has shattered

_____ 9. coagulates   I. soldiers who fight on foot

_____ 10. fragments   J. tight band used to stop bleeding

Prereading Vocabulary Worksheets *A Farewell to Arms*

Book Two: Chapters XIII-XVIII
Part I: Using Prior Knowledge and Contextual Clues
Below are the sentences in which the vocabulary words appear in the text. Read the sentence. Use any clues you can find in the sentence combined with your prior knowledge, and write what you think the underlined word means in the space provided.

1. The porter came out with them. He had ray mustaches, wore a doorman's cap and was in his shirt sleeves.

   _____

2. "She said you were domineering and rude."

   _____

3. He was very solemn and refrained from talking.

   _____

4. He was very solemn and refrained from talking.

   _____

5. The doctor requested me to write in his pocket notebook, my name, and regiment and some sentiment.

   _____

6. "Please move the knee," the bearded doctor said.
   "I can't."
   "Test the articulation?" the bearded doctor questioned.

   _____

7. "Certainly. It is a question of time, I could not conscientiously open a knee like that before the projectile was encysted."

   _____

Prereading Vocabulary Worksheets *A Farewell to Arms*
Book Two: Chapters XIII-XVIII Continued

8. "Certainly. It is a question of time, I could not conscientiously open a knee like that before the projectile was encysted."

_____

9. "Smooth as piano keys," and she would stroke my chin with her finger and say, "Smooth as emery paper and very hard on piano keys."

_____

10. I wanted to be really married but Catherine said that if we were they would send her away and if we merely started on the formalities they would watch her and would break us up.

_____

Part II: Determining the Meaning: Match the vocabulary words to their dictionary definitions.

_____ 1. porter   A. serious; humorless

_____ 2. domineering   B. thoughts based on feelings

_____ 3. solemn   C. carefully

_____ 4. refrained   D. official procedures

_____ 5. sentiment   E. bullet; shell

_____ 6. articulation   F. bossy or controlling

_____ 7. conscientiously G. connection; fitting together

_____ 8. projectile   H. sandpaper

_____ 9. emery   I. held back; kept from doing

_____ 10. formalities   J. employee who carries luggage

Prereading Vocabulary Worksheets *A Farewell to Arms*

Book Two: Chapters XIX-XXIV
Part I: Using Prior Knowledge and Contextual Clues
Below are the sentences in which the vocabulary words appear in the text. Read the sentence. Use any clues you can find in the sentence combined with your prior knowledge, and write what you think the underlined word means in the space provided.

1. They would not let us go out together when I was off crutches because it was unseemly for a nurse to be seen <u>unchaperoned</u> with a patient who did not look as though he needed attendance, so we were not together much in the afternoons.

___

2. "I do all right," Meyers said. He was being <u>cordial</u>. "You ought to come out."

___

3. "I hear you're going to get the silver medal," Ettore said to me. "What kind of <u>citation</u> you going to get?"

___

4. He was a <u>legitimate</u> hero who bored everyone he met.

___

5. "Wouldn't you like me to have some more <u>exalted</u> rank?"
"No, darling. I only want you to have enough rank so that we're admitted to the better restaurants."

___

6. "I'd have married you even if you were <u>conceited</u> but it's very restful to have a husband who's not conceited."

___

7. They all <u>squabbled</u> about divisions and only killed them when they got them.

___

Prereading Vocabulary Worksheets *A Farewell to Arms*
Book Two: Chapters XIX-XXIV Continued

8. "Nothing. I was only thinking how small obstacles seemed that once were so big."
_____

9. She seemed upset and taut.
_____

10. There were not enough places in the train and everyone was hostile. The machine-gunner stood up for me to sit down.

_____

Part II: Determining the Meaning: Match the vocabulary words to their dictionary definitions.

_____ 1. unchaperoned   A. unfriendly; showing hatred toward another

_____ 2. cordial   B. argued

_____ 3. citation   C. official document of praise

_____ 4. legitimate   D. pleasant, friendly

_____ 5. exalted   E. having a very high opinion of one-self

_____ 6. conceited   F. things that get in the way or stop progress

_____ 7. squabbled   G. praiseworthy

_____ 8. obstacles   H. not accompanied by a supervisor

_____ 9. taut   I. legal, lawful

_____ 10. hostile   J. tense

Prereading Vocabulary Worksheets *A Farewell to Arms*

Book Three: Chapters XXV-XXVII
Part I: Using Prior Knowledge and Contextual Clues
Below are the sentences in which the vocabulary words appear in the text. Read the sentence. Use any clues you can find in the sentence combined with your prior knowledge, and write what you think the underlined word means in the space provided.

1. I got down from the camion in the big square in front of the Town Major's house, the driver handed down my rucksack and I put it on and swing on the two musettes and walked to our villa.

   _____

2. "I know, you are the fine good Anglo-Saxon boy. I know. You are the remorse boy, I know. I will wait till I see the Anglo-Saxon brushing away harlotry with a toothbrush."

   _____

3. "I love you, baby," he said. "You puncture me when I become a great Italian thinker."

   _____

4. He acted very elated now.

   _____

5. Food was scarce and he would be glad to get a full meal in Gorizia.

   _____

6. I would recognize them because of their flat trajectory.

   _____

7. Abstract words such as glory, honor, courage, or hallow were obscene beside the concrete names of villages, the numbers of roads, the names of rivers, the numbers of regiments and the dates.

   _____

Prereading Vocabulary Worksheets *A Farewell to Arms*
Book Three: Chapters XXV-XXVII Continued

8. That night we helped empty the field hospitals that had been set up in the least ruined villages of the plateau, taking the wounded down to Plava on the river-bed: and the next day hauled all day in the rain to <u>evacuate</u> the hospitals and clearing station at Plava.

_____

9. "I'd like to have a crack at them for nothing. They charge too much at that house anyway. The government <u>gyps</u> us."

_____

10. "Beyond the Tagliamento, they say. The hospital and the <u>sector</u> are to be at the Pordenone."

_____

Part II: Determining the Meaning: Match the vocabulary words to their dictionary definitions.

_____ 1. rucksack   A. cheats out of money

_____ 2. remorse   B. in short supply; limited

_____ 3. puncture   C. strong feeling of guilt or sorrow

_____ 4. elated   D. route; path

_____ 5. scarce   E. zone; division

_____ 6. trajectory   F. morally offensive

_____ 7. obscene   G. backpack

_____ 8. evacuates   H. leaves a dangerous place

_____ 9. gyps   I. happy and excited

_____ 10. sector   J. reduce someone's confidence

Prereading Vocabulary Worksheets *A Farewell to Arms*

Book Three: Chapters XVIII-XXXII
Part I: Using Prior Knowledge and Contextual Clues
Below are the sentences in which the vocabulary words appear in the text. Read the sentence. Use any clues you can find in the sentence combined with your prior knowledge, and write what you think the underlined word means in the space provided.

1. "He's an anarchist," Piani said. "He doesn't go to church."

_____

2. "No, Tenente. We're socialists. We come from Imola."

_____

3. There were two windows in the roof, one was blocked with boards, the other was a narrow dormer window on the north side.

_____

4. We could pry a board loose and see out of the south window down into the courtyard.

_____

5. I was vague in the head from lying in the hay. I had nearly been asleep.

_____

6. There was no exhilaration in crossing the bridge.

_____

7. The officers were scrutinizing everyone in the column, sometimes speaking to each other, going forward to flash a light in someone's face.

_____

8. They were also dealing summarily with German agitators in Italian uniforms.

_____

Prereading Vocabulary Worksheets *A Farewell to Arms*
Book Three: Chapters XXVIII-XXXII Continued

9. They were also dealing summarily with German <u>agitators</u> in Italian uniforms.

_____

10. I stared at him <u>contemptuously</u> and he looked away.

_____

Part II: Determining the Meaning: Match the vocabulary words to their dictionary definitions.

_____ 1. anarchist   A. not clear in meaning

_____ 2. socialists   B. immediately

_____ 3. dormer   C. a person who thinks government should be abandoned

_____ 4. pry   D. a window built at right angles to the roof

_____ 5. vague   E. force open

_____ 6. exhilaration   F. happiness and excitement

_____ 7. scrutinizing   G. in a disapproving way

_____ 8. summarily   H. people who believe in control by the people

_____ 9. agitators   I. protesters

_____ 10. contemptuously   J. examining carefully

Prereading Vocabulary Worksheets *A Farewell to Arms*

Book Four: Chapters XXXIII-XXXVII
Part I: Using Prior Knowledge and Contextual Clues
Below are the sentences in which the vocabulary words appear in the text. Read the sentence. Use any clues you can find in the sentence combined with your prior knowledge, and write what you think the underlined word means in the space provided.

1. "Yes, I know that. But the Swiss. What will they do?"
   "They intern you."

   _____

2. It kills the very good and the very gentle and the very brave impartially.

   _____

3. He was living to be one hundred years old and played a smoothly fluent game of billiards that contrasted with his own ninety-four year old brittleness.

   _____

4. "Now that is the great fallacy; the wisdom of old men. They do not grow wise, they grow careful."

   _____

5. "Dear boy, that is not wisdom. That is cynicism."

   _____

6. "I might become very devout," I said. "Anyway, I will pray for you."

   _____

7. "Haven't you got an umbrella, sir?"
   "No, I said. "This coat sheds water."

   _____

8. I rowed in the dark keeping the wind in my face. The rain had stopped and only came occasionally in gusts.

   _____

Prereading Vocabulary Worksheets *A Farewell to Arms*
Book Four: Chapters XXXIII-XXXVII Continued

9. Then I began to catch crabs and soon I was just chopping along again with a thin brown taste of <u>bile</u> from having rowed too hard after the brandy.

_____

10. "It's all right, darling. Don't be upset. We'll get a good sleep and you won't feel <u>groggy</u> tomorrow."

_____

Part II: Determining the Meaning: Match the vocabulary words to their dictionary definitions.

_____ 1. intern   A. sudden violent burst of wind

_____ 2. impartially   B. fairly

_____ 3. brittleness   C. weak or dizzy

_____ 4. fallacy   D. a belief that is actually incorrect

_____ 5. cynicism   E. causes water to flow or drop off

_____ 6. devout   F. sarcasm; mocking

_____ 7. sheds   G. fluid produced in the liver

_____ 8. gusts   H. put in prison

_____ 9. bile   I. very religious

_____ 10. groggy   J. weak and likely to break or crack

Prereading Vocabulary Worksheets *A Farewell to Arms*

Book Five: Chapters XXXVIII-XLI
Part I: Using Prior Knowledge and Contextual Clues
Below are the sentences in which the vocabulary words appear in the text. Read the sentence. Use any clues you can find in the sentence combined with your prior knowledge, and write what you think the underlined word means in the space provided.

1. Outside, in front of the chalet a road went up the mountain.

_____

2. But we did not mind the hardness of the road because we had nails in the soles and heels of our boots and the heel nails bit on the frozen ruts and with nailed boots it was good walking on the road and invigorating.

_____

3. "I know one thing. I'm not going to be married in this splendidly matronly state."

_____

4. "It would be fun. I'm tired of it. It's an awful nuisance in the bed at night."

_____

5. It rained on all morning and turned the snow to slush and made the mountain-side dismal.

_____

6. The road was a torrent of muddy snow-water.

_____

7. "I'm just something very ungainly that you've married."

_____

8. "Do you wish to commence your dinner with soup?"

_____

Prereading Vocabulary Worksheets *A Farewell to Arms*
Book Five: Chapters 38-41 XXXVIII-XLI Continued

9. "The first labor is usually <u>protracted</u>," the nurse said.

_____

10. "Hello, darling," Catherine said in a <u>strained</u> voice. "I'm not doing much."

_____

Part II: Determining the Meaning: Match the vocabulary words to their dictionary definitions.

_____ 1. chalet   A. begin

_____ 2. invigorating   B. clumsy; not graceful

_____ 3. matronly   C. gloomy; depressing to look at

_____ 4. nuisance   D. annoyance; irritation

_____ 5. dismal   E. full of tension; nervous

_____ 6. torrent   F. lasting for a long time

_____ 7. ungainly   G. a woman with mature, sensible qualities

_____ 8. commence   H. filling with energy

_____ 9. protracted   I. traditional Swiss wooden cottage

_____ 10. strained   J. fast, powerful flood of water

DAILY LESSON PLANS

LESSON ONE

Objectives
1. To introduce the *A Farewell To Arms* unit
2. To distribute books, study guides and other related materials
3. To give students background information about Hemingway and his works

Activity #1

Distribute books, study guides, and reading assignments. Explain in detail how students are to use these materials.

Study Guides Students should preview the study guide questions before each reading assignment to get a feeling for what events and ideas are important in that section. After reading the section, students will (as a class or individually) answer the question to review the important events and ideas from that section of the book. Students should keep the study guides as study materials for the unit test.

Reading/Writing Assignment Sheet You (the teachers) need to fill in the reading and writing assignment sheet to let students know when their reading has to be completed. You can either write the assignment sheet on a side blackboard or bulletin board and leave it there for students to see each day, or you can duplicate copies for each student to have. In either case, you should advise students to become very familiar with the reading assignments so they know what is expected of them.

Unit Outline You may find it helpful to distribute copies of the Unit Outline to your students so they can keep track of upcoming lessons and assignments. You may also want to post a copy of the Unit Outline on a bulletin board and cross off each lesson as you complete it.

Extra Activities Center The Unit Resource Materials portion of this unit contains suggestions for a library of related books and articles in your classroom as well as crossword and word search puzzles. Make an extra activities center in your classroom where you will keep these materials for students to use. Bring the books and articles in from the library and keep several copies of the puzzles on hand. Explain to students that these materials are available for students to use when they finish reading assignments or other class work early.

Books Each school has its own rules and regulations regarding student use of school books. Advise students of the procedures that are normal for your school.

Notebook or Unit Folder You may want the students to keep all of their worksheets, notes, and other papers for the unit together in a binder or notebook. During the first class meeting, tell them how you want them to arrange the folder. Make divider pages for vocabulary worksheets, Prereading study guide questions, review activities, notes, and tests. You may want to give a grade for accuracy in keeping the folder.

Lesson One, continued

Activity #2
    Show a film about Hemingway and his works. A&E's Biography video for Hemingway is available on Amazon.com. The worksheet which follows is based on that video. The purposes of the worksheet are to keep students' attention on the film, to provide students with a guide to the points you want them to remember, and to give students a good study guide for the background information.

Activity #3
    Discuss the answers to the worksheet in the remaining time.

FILL IN THE BLANKS
To Go With A&E Biography Video About
Ernest Hemingway

Hemingway was born on July 21, _____. Hemingway's uncle helped get him his first job at the *Kansas City* _____. In 1917 Hemingway was rejected by the army because of poor vision, and volunteered for the _____ _____ ambulance division in Italy. While in Italy, Hemingway was wounded and fell in love with his nurse, _____, in Milan. After he returned to America, she sent him a letter ending the relationship. He met and married _____ Richardson, the love of his life. He got a job as a foreign correspondent for the *Star* and moved to Paris, where he met Gertrude _____, who helped him and influenced his writing. She said of Hemingway and others like him, "That's what you are; that's what you all are, you young people who served in the war; you are a _____ _____." Hemingway's motto in writing was to hone the work to the essence of the idea: to write one _____ sentence. In December 1922 Hadley lost all except three of Hemingway's _____ on her trip to visit him in Paris. In 1923, Hemingway traveled to _____ and was introduced to bullfighting. Shortly after, his first son, _____, was born. Published in 1926, The _____ was Hemingway's break-through book. It was both a critical and commercial success. Shortly after the publication of this book, a friend of the Hemingways, _____ Pfeiffer practically moved in with them. She was more cosmopolitan than Hadley, and Hemingway fell in love with her. He divorced Hadley and married Pauline, though he still cared for Hadley and John. He dedicated The Sun Also Rises to them and gave them the proceeds from that novel. In 1928 Hemingway left Paris and moved to _____ _____. The first novel he wrote there was ____ _____ _____ _____, about his service in Italy and romance with Agnes. The world was introduced to the Hemingway code of _____ under pressure. Hemingway's _____, Ed, committed suicide while Hemingway was writing A Farewell To Arms. Shortly before Ed's death, Hemingway's second son, _____, was born. Three years later, his third son, _____ was born. Hemingway has spurts of being a good _____, but when he was not in a fatherly mode, his children were not a part of his life. Hemingway's second book written in Key West, _____ _____ _____ _____, was a tribute to bullfighting. In 1933 Hemingway went on a hunting safari in Africa. While there, he saw Mt. _____ which later became part of his book _____ _____ ____ _____. In 1935 Hemingway's personal account of big game hunting, _____ _____ _____ ___ _____ was published. Because of health reasons, Hemingway's wife, Pauline, couldn't have any more _____. Hemingway had an affair with a woman named _____ _____. After his affair with Jane ended, he met _____ _____ Gelhorn in Key West. Hemingway married her a few weeks after his divorce from Pauline, and they moved to _____. In Cuba, he wrote _____ _____ _____ _____ _____, Hemingway's grim portrayal of the Spanish Civil War. Martha was a _____, too. She became a war correspondent and covered the war in Europe. Hemingway didn't like having professional competition from his wife, and she didn't like the way he treated her. The end of World _____ II marked the end of their relationship. Hemingway next married _____ _____ in 1946. She was a writer, too, but never let her professional career shine above Hemingway's. In the late 1940s through the early 1950s, several things happened in Hemingway's life. His son _____ was injured in a car accident. His mother, _____, his former wife, _____, Max _____, and Mr. _____ all died. His next book, Across the _____ and into the _____, was a critical failure. However, he came back with what some consider his best work ever, The _____ _____ and the _____, for which he won a Pulitzer Prize in 1953. In 1954 Hemingway was involved in two _____ crashes. In the second one, he was seriously injured. While recovering from the second crash, he was awarded the _____ Prize for literature. In 1960 Hemingway left Cuba, moved to Idaho, and wrote A Moveable _____, which was about his early years in Paris. His health was deteriorating due to his heavy _____ and the many injuries and illnesses he had had during his adventures. In 1960 he was diagnosed with _____, for which the treatment was electric shocks. After several treatments and the resulting loss of memory, Hemingway was unable to _____. He committed _____ in his home in Ketchum. Hemingway's style was _____ and his _____ were broad: courage, _____ under pressure, and characters being transformed by a _____ or loss. His writing style can be summed up in his own words, "Write one true _____."

FILL IN THE BLANKS ANSWER KEY
To Go With A&E Biography Video About
Ernest Hemingway

Hemingway was born on July 21, **1899**. Hemingway's uncle helped get him his first job at the *Kansas City **Star***. In 1917 Hemingway was rejected by the army because of poor vision, and volunteered for the **Red Cross** ambulance division in Italy. While in Italy, Hemingway was wounded and fell in love with his nurse, **Agnes von Kurowsky**, in Milan. After he returned to America, she sent him a letter ending the relationship. He met and married **Hadley** Richardson, the love of his life. He got a job as a foreign correspondent for the *Star* and moved to Paris, where he met Gertrude **Stein**, who helped him and influenced his writing. She said of Hemingway and others like him, "That's what you are; that's what you all are, you young people who served in the war; you are a **Lost Generation**." Hemingway's motto in writing was to hone the work to the essence of the idea: write one true sentence. In December 1922 Hadley lost all except three of Hemingway's **manuscripts** on her trip to visit him in Paris. In 1923, Hemingway traveled to **Spain** and was introduced to bullfighting. Shortly after, his first son, **John Hadley Nicanor Hemingway**, was born. Published in 1926, *The **Sun Also Rises*** was Hemingway's break-through book. It was both a critical and commercial success. Shortly after the publication of this book, a friend of the Hemingways, **Pauline** Pfeiffer practically moved in with them. She was more cosmopolitan than Hadley, and Hemingway fell in love with her. He divorced Hadley and married Pauline, though he still cared for Hadley and John. He dedicated *The Sun Also Rises* to them and gave them the proceeds from that novel. In 1928 Hemingway left Paris and moved to **Key West**. The first novel he wrote there was ***A Farewell To Arms***, about his service in Italy and romance with Agnes. The world was introduced to the Hemingway code of **grace** under pressure. Hemingway's **father**, Ed, committed suicide while Hemingway was writing *A Farewell To Arms*. Shortly before Ed's death, Hemingway's second son, **Patrick**, was born. Three years later, his third son, **Gregory** was born. Hemingway has spurts of being a good **father**, but when he was not in a fatherly mode, his children were not a part of his life. Hemingway's second book written in Key West, ***Death in the Afternoon***, was a tribute to bullfighting. In 1933 Hemingway went on a hunting safari in Africa. While there, he saw Mt. **Kilimanjaro**, which later became part of his book ***The Snows of Kilimanjaro***. In 1935 Hemingway's personal account of big game hunting, ***The Green Hills of Africa***, was published.

Because of health reasons, Hemingway's wife, Pauline, couldn't have any more **children**. Hemingway had an affair with a woman named **Jane Mason**. After his affair with Jane ended, he met **Martha Gelhorn** in Key West. Hemingway married her a few weeks after his divorce from Pauline, and they moved to **Cuba**. In Cuba, he wrote ***For Whom The Bell Tolls***, Hemingway's grim portrayal of the Spanish Civil War. Martha was a **writer**, too. She became a war correspondent and covered the war in Europe. Hemingway didn't like having professional competition from his wife, and she didn't like the way he treated her. The end of World **War** II marked the end of their relationship. Hemingway next married **Mary Welsh** in 1946. She was a writer, too, but never let her professional career shine above Hemingway's. In the late 1940s through the early 1950s, several things happened in Hemingway's life. His son **Patrick** was injured in a car accident. His mother, **Grace**, his former wife, **Pauline**, Max **Eastman**, and Mr. **Scribner** all died. His next book, *Across the **River** and into the **Tree***, was a critical failure. However, he came back with what some consider his best work ever, *The **Old Man** and the **Sea***, for which he won a Pulitzer Prize in 1953. In 1954 Hemingway was involved in two **plane** crashes. In the second one, he was seriously injured. While recovering from the second crash, he was awarded the **Nobel** Prize for literature. In 1960 Hemingway left Cuba, moved to Idaho, and wrote *A Moveable **Feast***, which was about his early years in Paris. His health was deteriorating due to his heavy **drinking** and the many injuries and illnesses he had had during his adventures. In 1960 he was diagnosed with **depression**, for which the treatment was electric shocks. After several treatments and the resulting loss of memory, Hemingway was unable to **write**. He committed **suicide** in his home in Ketchum. Hemingway's style was **minimal** and his **themes** were broad: courage, **grace** under pressure, and characters being transformed by a **challenge** or loss. His writing style can be summed up in his own words, "Write one true **sentence**."

LESSON TWO

Objectives
1. To do the prereading work for Book One, Chapters I-VII
2. To read Book One, Chapters I-VII
3. To become acquainted with the Nonfiction Assignment

Activity #1
Show students how to preview the study questions and do the vocabulary work for Chapters I-VII. Encourage students to take notes as they read. If students own their books, encourage them to use highlighters or colored pens to mark important passages and the answers to the study guide questions.

Activity #2
Read Chapter I aloud to students to set the mood for the novel. Then have students read Chapters II-VII orally. Either call on students or ask for volunteers, whichever works best with your class. Be sure to give students who need practice reading orally the opportunity to do so, even if it slows down the reading schedule a little. If you have not given students a grade for oral reading this quarter, during the reading of this novel would be a good time to grade them. Be sure to let them know that they will be evaluated and tell them the criteria you will use.

If students do not complete reading this assignment in class, they should finish it on their own time prior to the next class period.

Activity #3
Distribute copies of the Nonfiction Assignment Sheet and go over it in detail with the students. Explain to students that they each are to read at least one nonfiction piece at some time during the unit. This could be a book, a magazine article, or information from an encyclopedia or the Internet. Students will fill out a Nonfiction Assignment Sheet after completing the reading to help you (the teacher) evaluate their reading experiences and to help the students think about and evaluate their own reading. Encourage students to read about topics that are related to the theme of the novel.

NONFICTION ASSIGNMENT SHEET *A Farewell to Arms*
(To be completed after reading the required nonfiction article.)

Name _____ Date _____ Class _____

Title of Nonfiction Read _____

Written by _____ Publication Date _____

Web Site Address (if applicable) _____

I. Factual Summary: Write a summary of the piece you read.

II. Vocabulary:
    1. Which vocabulary words were difficult?

    2. What did you do to help yourself understand the words?

III. Interpretation: What was the main point the author wanted you to get from reading his/her work?

IV. Criticism:
    1. Which points of the piece did you agree with or find easy to believe? Why?

    2. With which points of the piece did you disagree or find difficult to believe? Why?

V. Personal Response:
    1. What did you think about this piece?

    2. How does this piece help you understand the novel *A Farewell to Arms*?

LESSON THREE

Objectives
1. To review the main ideas and events from Book One, Chapters I-VII
2. To do the prereading work for Book One, Chapters VIII-XII
2. To give students the opportunity to practice reading orally
3. To give the teacher the opportunity to evaluate students' reading skills

Activity #1
Give students time to answer the study guide questions from Book One, Chapters I-VII and then discuss the answers in detail. Write the answers on the board or overhead projector film so students can have the correct answers for study purposes.

Note: It is a good practice in public speaking and leadership skills for individual students to take charge of leading the discussion of the study questions. Perhaps a different student could go to the front of the class and lead the discussion each day that the study questions are discussed during the unit.

Activity #2
Give students about ten or fifteen minutes to complete the Prereading vocabulary worksheet and preview the study guide questions for Chapters VIII-XII.

Activity #3
Tell students their oral reading ability will be evaluated. Show them copies of the Oral Reading Evaluation form and discuss it. Model correct intonation and expression by reading the first few paragraphs of Chapter VIII aloud.

Activity #4
Call on individual students to read a few paragraphs aloud. Encourage the other students to follow along in their books. If you have a student who is unwilling or unable to read aloud in front of the group, make arrangements to do his or her evaluation privately at another time. Mark the oral reading evaluation forms as the students read. If all students have read orally before the chapters have been completed, assign the remainder of the text as individual silent reading.

ORAL READING EVALUATION *A Farewell to Arms*

Name _____ Class _____ Date _____

SKILL	EXCELLENT	GOOD	AVERAGE	FAIR	POOR
FLUENCY	5	4	3	2	1
CLARITY	5	4	3	2	1
AUDIBILITY	5	4	3	2	1
PRONUNCIATION	5	4	3	2	1
_____	5	4	3	2	1
_____	5	4	3	2	1
TOTAL GRADE	5	4	3	2	1

COMMENTS:

LESSON FOUR

Objectives
1. To review the main events and ideas in Book One, Chapters VIII-XII
2. To write to express a personal opinion
3. To get the students to think about what "war" means
4. To give the teacher the opportunity to evaluate students' writing

Activity #1
   Have partners answer the study guide questions and review their prereading vocabulary worksheets. Go over the answers with the class. Then have partners write a few additional questions about the chapters. Have each pair read their questions aloud to the class and call on other students to answer.

Activity #2
   Distribute Writing Assignment #1 and discuss the directions in detail. Allow students the remainder of the class period to work on this assignment. Give students an additional two or three class periods to complete the assignment if necessary.

Activity #3
   Distribute copies of the Writing Evaluation Form (included in this Lit Plan.) Explain to students that during Lesson Nine you will be holding individual writing conferences about this writing assignment. Make sure they are familiar with the criteria on the Writing Evaluation Form.

WRITING ASSIGNMENT #1 *A Farewell To Arms*

PROMPT
Many passages in *A Farewell To Arms* describe war and its effects. Your assignment is to describe war in your own way. You may use any literary form you choose: a short story, a poem, an essay, a letter -- any form you think you could best use to give an accurate description of war. You may choose any point of view and any setting you wish. Be creative. Be accurate. Convey feelings and images. The emphasis of this assignment is to see how well you can describe something--in this case, war.

PREWRITING
Remember that a personal opinion piece can and should include your thoughts and feelings. As often as possible, support these thoughts and feelings with factual evidence or examples.

First, read the passages in *A Farewell to Arms* that describe war and its effects. If you own the book, you may want to highlight these passages in a certain color. Or, put sticky-notes next to the passages.

Then, read other descriptions of war. You may also want to watch a movie or television show about war to get a visual idea of its effects. There are several accurate presentations on Public Television and the History Channel. If possible, interview someone who has witnessed war, either as a soldier or civilian. If you do this, be sensitive in your questioning.

Make a concept web with the word "war" in the center. Around the center, write any words or phrases that remind you of war. Use this web as you write.

DRAFTING
Choose the literary form and point of view you want to use. Refer to the concept web you developed as you write. Write your first draft. Check to make sure you are including your opinion. Use as many descriptive words and images as you can. You may want to use a thesaurus to help you get a variety of words and their exact meanings.

PEER EDITING
When you finish the rough draft of your personal opinion piece, ask another student to read it. After reading your rough draft, the student should tell you what he/she liked best about your work, which parts were difficult to understand, and ways in which your work could be improved. Your reader should also be able to summarize your opinion about war based on your text. Reread your text considering your critic's comments, and make the revisions you think are necessary.

PROOFREADING
Do a final proofreading of your opinion piece, double checking your grammar, spelling, organization, and the clarity of your ideas. Revise as necessary before submitting it for grading.

WRITING EVALUATION FORM *A Farewell to Arms*

Name _____ Date _____ Class _____

Writing Assignment # _____

Circle One for Each Item:

Composition	Excellent	Good	Fair	Poor
Style	Excellent	Good	Fair	Poor
Grammar	Excellent	Good	Fair	Poor
Spelling	Excellent	Good	Fair	Poor
Punctuation	Excellent	Good	Fair	Poor
Legibility	Excellent	Good	Fair	Poor

Strengths:

Weaknesses:

Comments/Suggestions:

LESSON FIVE

Objectives
1. To complete the prereading work for Book Two, Chapters XIII-XVIII
2. To read Book Two, Chapters XIII-XVIII
3. To review the main ideas and events in Book Two, Chapters XIII-XVIII

Activity #1
Give students about ten minutes to do the prereading and vocabulary work for Chapters XIII-XVIII.

Activity #2
Have students read Chapters XIII-XVIII orally in class. Either call on students or ask for volunteers, whichever method works best. Students may enjoy taking the roles of the characters and the narrator and reading aloud.

Activity #3
If there is time at the end of the class period, have students work with partners to answer the study guide questions. Assign any remaining study guide questions to be completed before the next class period.

LESSON SIX

Objectives
    1. To complete the prereading work for Book Two, Chapters XIX-XXIV
    2. To read Book Two, Chapters XIX-XXIV in class
    3. To review the main ideas and events in Book Two, Chapters XIX-XXIV

Activity #1
    Give students about ten minutes to do the prereading and vocabulary work for Chapters XIX-XXIV. Have them work in small groups. Groups can divide the vocabulary words among the members and then share their definitions. A group leader can then read aloud the study guide questions and have students tell what they think will happen in the chapters.

Activity #2
    Have students begin read Chapters XIX-XXIV silently in class. Tell students that they should complete reading through Chapter XXIV prior to the next class period.

Activity #3
    Have the same small groups go over the answers to the study guide questions together. Provide assistance as necessary.

Activity #4
    Tell students they will have a quiz on Chapters XIII- XXIV during the next class period. Suggest that they make sure they have the answers to all of the prereading vocabulary worksheets and the study guide questions.

LESSON SEVEN

Objectives
1. To take a quiz on the main ideas and events of
   Book Two, Chapters XIII- XXIV
2. To participate in a writing conference with the teacher
3. To complete the prereading work for Book Three, Chapters XXV-XXVII
4. To read Book Three, Chapters XXV-XXVII

Activity #1

Quiz—Distribute quizzes (multiple choice study guide questions for Chapters XIII - XVIII and XIX-XXIV) and give students about twenty minutes to complete them. Correct and grade the papers as a class. You may want to have students exchange papers, or allow them to correct their own work. As an extra credit assignment, have students find the correct answers to any question they missed, and rewrite any "false" answers to be true. Collect the quizzes to record the grades.

Activity #2

Call students to your desk or to some other private area of the classroom. Discuss their papers from Writing Assignment #1. Use the completed Writing Evaluation form as a basis for your critique.

Activity #3

Students should use the class time when they are not conferencing with you to do any of the following: work on their nonfiction reading assignment; revise Writing Assignment #1; complete the prereading work for Chapters XXV-XXVII; read those chapters; or review the study guide questions and prereading vocabulary worksheets they have completed so far.

LESSON EIGHT

Objectives
1. To review the main ideas and events from Book Three, Chapters XXV-XXVII
2. To complete the prereading work for Book Three, Chapters XXVIII-XXXII
3. To read Book Three, Chapters XXVIII-XXXII

Activity #1
    Give students time to answer the study guide questions from Book Three, Chapters XXV-XXVII and then discuss the answers in detail. Write the answers on the board or overhead projector film so students can have the correct answers for study purposes.

Activity #2
    Give students about ten or fifteen minutes to complete the Prereading vocabulary worksheet and preview the study guide questions for Chapters XXVIII-XXXII.

Activity
    Have students read Chapters XXVIII-XXXII either orally or silently (your choice). If students do not complete this assignment in class, they should finish it on their own prior to the next class period.

LESSON NINE

Objectives
> 1. To review the main ideas and events from Book Three, Chapters XXVIII-XXXII
> 2. To exercise and expand students' composition skills, specifically those relating to sentence structure

Activity #1
> Have students sit in small groups to answer the study guide questions. Tell each group to choose a spokesperson. Discuss the answers to the study guide questions with the class, having each spokesperson respond for their group.

Activity #2
> NOTE: This assignment can be done either orally as a group or individually as a written assignment, whichever you prefer. Give students a brief review of sentence structure and ways of combining clauses into sentences. Then, have students look at the first two paragraphs of Chapter XXVIII. The sentences in these paragraphs could be combined in a number of different ways. Have students choose one or two sentences and rewrite them using a variety of sentence structures without changing the meaning. Ask students to write the original sentence in one color on chart paper and then write their revision under it in another color. Discuss with the class how the sentence structure affects their understanding of the meaning.

LESSON TEN

Objectives
> 1. To practice writing to persuade
> 2. To think more in-depth about one event of the novel
> 3. To practice thinking logically
> 4. To consider two different viewpoints of the same event

Activity #1
> Distribute Writing Assignment #2. Discuss the directions in detail and give students ample time to complete the assignment.

WRITING ASSIGNMENT #2 A *Farewell to Arms*

PROMPT

At the end of Book Three Chapter XXX, Frederick Henry deserts the Italian army by jumping into the river and swimming away. For the sake of this writing assignment, suppose that you are a friend of Frederick Henry's and you are opposed to his desertion. Write a letter from you to Frederick Henry and try to persuade him to go back to the army.

PREWRITING

Make a list of reasons that Frederick Henry should go back to the Italian army. Think of statements to support each of the reasons and list them under each reason. Then number the reasons in order from most to least important.

DRAFTING

Make an introductory paragraph in which you briefly recap the problem (Henry's desertion) and state your intent to persuade Henry to rejoin the army.

Then use one paragraph for each of the reasons that you have for suggesting that Frederick Henry go back in the army. Use the supporting statements for each reason.

Summarize your ideas and ask Frederick Henry to respond to you in writing.

PEER CONFERENCEING/REVISING

When you finish this rough draft, ask another student to look at it. You may want to give the student your prewriting checklist so he/she can double check for you and see that you have included all of the reasons and supporting statements. After reading, he/she should tell you what e/she liked best about your persuasive letter, which parts were difficult to understand or needed more information, and ways in which your work could be improved. Reread your persuasive letter considering your critic's comments and make the corrections you think are necessary.

PROOFREADING/EDITING

Do a final proofreading of your persuasive letter, double-checking your grammar, spelling, organization, and the clarity of your ideas.

FINAL DRAFT

Follow your teacher's guidelines for completing the final draft of your letter.

LESSON ELEVEN

Objectives
1. To complete the prereading work for Book Four, Chapters XXXIII-XXXVII
2. To read Book Four, Chapters XXXIII-XXXVII
3. To review the main ideas and events from Book Four, Chapters XXXIII-XXXVII

Activity #1
Give students about ten minutes to complete the prereading work for Chapters XXXIII-XXXVII.

Activity #2
Have students read chapters XXXIII-XXXVII silently in class.

Activity #3
Tell students to begin answering the study guide questions for Chapters XXXIII-XXXVII when they finish the reading. Remind them that if they do not finish in class, the work will be due for the next class period.

LESSON TWELVE

1. To make predictions about how the novel will end
2. To complete the prereading work for Book Five, Chapters XXXVIII-XLI
3. To read Book Five, Chapters XXXVIII-XLI
4. To review the main ideas and events from Book Five, Chapters XXXVIII-XLI

Activity #1

Before students read the study guide questions or the chapter, have them write down a prediction about how they think the story will end. Allow about ten minutes for students to discuss their predictions in small groups. Ask students to hold onto the papers where they wrote their predictions until they have finished reading the last few chapters.

Activity #2

Give students about ten minutes to complete the prereading work for Chapters XXXVIII-XLI.

Activity #3

Have small groups read the chapters aloud together. They can either assign roles as was done in Lesson Five, or they can each read a paragraph or a few pages.

Activity #4

Have students work in the same small groups to answer the study guide questions. Then go over the answers with the whole class.

Activity #5

Ask students to get out their predictions again. Ask for a show of hands for the number of students who correctly predicted the ending. Invite students to explain what led them to make the predictions that they made.

LESSON THIRTEEN

Objectives
1. To arrive at a definition of Hemingway's "code hero"
2. To investigate *A Farewell to Arms* for characteristics of Frederick Henry and Catherine Barkley to determine the degree to which each is a "code hero"
3. To share conclusions with the class

Activity #1
Ask students for their definitions of the word "hero." Write the characteristics they suggest on the board. Then explain that Hemingway had his own ideas about what a hero should be.

Activity #2
Give students the characteristics of Hemingway's code hero. Write them on the board and explain each one. Students should copy this information into their notes.

Activity #3
Divide the class into groups of five students. Assign each group to study Frederick Henry or Catherine. Explain that students are to work together to find characteristics of Frederick or Catherine in order to determine the degree to which each is a Hemingway "code hero." Each of the students in the group should investigate one book of the novel. Each should jot down examples from his section of the novel showing his group's character demonstrating the characteristics of a "code hero." Students will then compare and share notes, working together to determine the degree to which the group's character is a complete Hemingway "code hero."

Activity #4
Have each group report its findings orally. Discuss the characteristics as necessary and make a list of the findings on the board for students to copy. Also compare and contrast Catherine and Frederick as code heroes.

A FEW NOTES ABOUT HEMINGWAY'S CODE HERO

Hemingway created a new type of character in his novels. This character appealed to the readers of the 1920s, when Hemingway first became popular. Many of the readers were able to identify with this hero, although sometimes as a fantasy portrayal of what the typical male wanted to be or do. Usually a male character, he was portrayed as a real "man's man." In time, this character became known as the "code hero."

Note: In a few cases, a female character also had the characteristics of the code hero. This is true of Catherine Barkley in *A Farwell to Arms*.

The Hemingway hero:
- a. Is a man of action, not talk
- b. Believes that death is the total end of life
- c. Lives a life full of sensuous pleasures (drinking, eating, making love)
- d. Has courage and shows grace under pressure
- e. Will often stay awake at night and sleep during the day
- f. Values order and self-discipline
- g. Controls his emotions
- h. Is very skillful at some work
- i. Often dislikes people who do not possess self-discipline or competence
- j. Is loyal to a small group of people

LESSON FOURTEEN

Objective
To discuss *A Farewell To Arms* more completely

Activity
Use the Extra Writing Assignments/Discussions Questions as a springboard for discussing the novel in more depth. Either write answers to the questions on the board or simply have students take notes during the discussion. NOTE: This is a good time to combine activities to have students practice note-taking skills. If time permits (or if you can make time), allow students to just take notes during the discussion. You should take notes answering the questions on an overhead projector transparency during the discussion, as if you were answering the questions on the board for students to copy. Leave the projector off during the discussion. When the discussion is complete, go back, turn on the projector and briefly review the ideas students should have written into their notes. Allow time for students to fix their notes so they have all the information you want them to have. (Save your transparency for the next time you do the unit.)

EXTRA WRITING ASSIGNMENTS / DISCUSSION QUESTIONS
A Farewell To Arms

<u>Interpretive</u>

1. Title each of the five books of the novel and explain your choices.

2. Suppose Frederick Henry would tell about the events of this story a few years after it happened. What do you think he would say?

3. Look back to Chapter I and find how many symbols and ideas for the novel were introduced there.

4. Discuss the significance of the places where other people want Frederick Henry to go on vacation.

5. Compare and contrast Rinaldi's visit to Frederick Henry in the hospital with the priest's.

6. There are many references to religious symbols, traditional symbols of good and evil. For example, in Chapter I, the plains (symbolic of temptation or "bad" in the novel) were rich with fruit trees (the apple fruit being traditionally associated with temptation); Rinaldi (one who lives by the pleasures of life) calls himself the snake (traditionally a symbol of\ temptation or evil). What other symbols of this type can you find in the novel?

7. Frederick Henry is an atheist, but he respects the priest. Why?

8. All along the way of the story, there are people who help Catherine and Frederick. Who are they, and what does each contribute?

9. Hemingway sneaks in many details in his descriptions and dialogues. Find examples of the following throughout the novel: a. Attitude towards the war and Italian army; b. Not thinking about or not talking about something; c. The idea of having a home; d. The idea that death is the end of all life ; e. Mountains as "good"; plains as "bad."

10. Discuss the opposite influences of Rinaldi and the priest on Frederick.

11. Discuss Catherine's influence on Frederick.

12. Plot Frederick's growth as a character through the novel.

13. Discuss the weather and seasons as they relate to the events in the novel.

14. How much time passes during the story?

15. Describe the retreat and explain its effect on Frederick Henry.

Daily Lesson Plans *A Farewell to Arms*

Extra Writing Assignment/Discussion Questions, Continued

16. Explain the significance of the title of the novel.

17. Explain the symbolic importance of Frederick's escape in the river.

Critical

18. What effect does the fact that Frederick Henry is the first-person narrator have on the story?

19. Is the story of *A Farewell To Arms* believable? Explain why or why not.

20. In the very first sentence, Hemingway introduces the house looking across the river and plain to the mountains. Explain the symbolic significance of this passage.

21. Are the characters in *A Farewell To Arms* stereotypes? If so, explain the usefulness of employing stereotypes in *A Farewell To Arms*. If they are not, explain how they merit individuality.

22. Describe Hemingway's writing style.

23. Discuss the symbolic meaning of rain, Catherine's long hair, Frederick's beard, nighttime, and food.

24. Explain how *A Farewell To Arms* is a tragedy.

25. Is this conclusion of the story inevitable?

26. What purpose does Catherine's death serve?

Personal Response

27. Imitate Hemingway's writing style as you write a story about something which has recently happened to you or an event which has recently taken place at school.

28. Define the word "hero."

29. Choose one scene from A Farewell To Arms and write it as a play. Then, explain the difficulties, if any, you encountered in doing so.

30. Write a parody of *A Farewell To Arms*.

Daily Lesson Plans *A Farewell to Arms*

Extra Writing Assignment/Discussion Questions, Continued

31. Do you agree or disagree with the philosophy of life, which Hemingway sets forth through the "code hero"?

32. Some critics think Hemingway was a great writer. Others say too much is made of his works. What do you think?

33. Explain why *A Farewell To Arms* would have been popular to Hemingway's audience in 1929.

QUOTATIONS

Discuss the significance of the following quotations from the book. The chapter number and speaker are given.

1. In the late summer of that year we lived in a house in a village that looked across the river and the plain to the mountains. (I)

2. The plain was rich with crops; there were many orchards of fruit trees and beyond the plain the mountains were brown and bare. (I)

3. This was a game, like bridge, in which you said things instead of playing cards . . .. Nobody had mentioned what the stakes were. It was alright with me. (Frederick, VI)

4. Well, I knew I would not be killed. Not in this war. It did not have anything to do with me. It seemed no more dangerous to me myself than war in the movies. (Frederick, VII)

5. "We think. We read. We are not peasants. We are mechanics. But even the peasants know better than to believe in a war. Everybody hates this war." (Passini, IX)

6. "There is a class that controls a country that is stupid and does not realize anything and never can. That is why we have this war." (Frederick, IX)

7. "You rank as an officer. I am an officer." (Frederick to Priest)
"I am not really. You are not even an Italian. You are a foreigner." (Priest to Frederick)
"You should be respected." (Frederick to Priest) (XI)

8. "Well, if I ever get it I will tell you." (Frederick, XI)

9. He had a rotten life in the mess and he was fine about it but I thought how he would be in his own country. (XI)

Daily Lesson Plans *A Farewell to Arms*

Quotations, Continued

10. I have noticed that doctors who fail in the practice of medicine have a tendency to seek one another's company and aid in consultation. (XV)

11. "You'll die then. Fight or die. That's what people do. They don't marry." (Catherine, XVII)

12. "What good would it do to marry now? We're really married. I couldn't be any more married." (Catherine, XVIII)

13. "You're my religion. You're all I've got." (Catherine, XVIII)

14. "I'll have to go back to the front pretty soon." (Frederick, XVIII)
    "We won't think about that until you go." (Catherine, XVIII)

15. He was a legitimate hero who bored every one he met. Catherine could not stand him. (XIX)

16. "No, darling. I only want you to have enough rank so that we're admitted to the better restaurants." (Catherine, XIX)

17. "I'm afraid of the rain because sometimes I see me dead in it." (Catherine, XIX)

18. ". . . I can keep you safe. I know I can. But nobody can help themselves." (Catherine, XIX)

19. He said we were all cooked but we were all right as long as we did not know it. We were all cooked. The thing was not to recognize it. The last country to realize they were cooked would win the war. (XXI)

20. But life isn't hard to manage when you've nothing to lose. (XXI)

21. " . . . there's only us two and in the world there's all the rest of them. If anything comes between us we're gone and then they have us."(Catherine, XXI)

22. The brave dies perhaps two thousand deaths if he's intelligent. He simply doesn't mention them. (XXI)

23. "I never felt like a whore before . . . . I'm a good girl again . . . . I wish we could do something really sinful. Everything we do seems so innocent and simple. I can't believe we do anything wrong." (Catherine, XXIII)

Daily Lesson Plans *A Farewell to Arms*

Quotations, Continued

24. "I am very tired of this war. If I was away I do not believe I would come back." (Signor Maggiore, XXV)

25. "I am the snake. I am the snake of reason." (Rinaldi, XXV)

26. Abstract words such as glory, honor, courage or hallow were obscene beside the concrete names of villages, the numbers of roads, the names of rivers, the numbers of regiments and the dates. (XXVII)

27. You see we don't believe in the war anyway, Tenente. (Piani, XXX)

28. If they shot floorwalkers after a fire in the department store because they spoke with an accent they had always had, then certainly the floorwalkers would not be expected to return when the store opened again for business. (XXXII)

29. Anger was washed away in the river along with any obligation. (XXXII)

30. I was going to forget the war. I had made a separate peace. (XXXIV)

31. Don't talk about the war. The war was a long way away. Maybe there wasn't any war. There was no war here. Then I realized it was over for me. But I did not have the feeling that it was really over. I had the feeling of a boy who thinks of what is happening at a certain hour at the schoolhouse from which he has played truant. (XXXIV)

32. You have no shame and no honor and you're as sneaky as he is. (Miss Ferguson, XXXIV)

33. If people bring so much courage to this world the world has to kill them to break them, so of course it kills them . . . . It kills the very good and the very gentle and the very brave impartially. (XXXIV)

34. "Darling, please be sensible. It's not deserting from the army. It's only the Italian army." (Catherine, XXXIV)

35. "My life used to be full of everything. Now if you aren't with me I haven't a thing in the world." (Catherine, XXXV)

36. "Dear boy, that's not wisdom. That is cynicism." (Count Greffi, XXXV)

37. "Then too you are in love. Do not forget that is a religious feeling." (Count Greffi, XXXV)

Daily Lesson Plans *A Farewell to Arms*

Quotations, Continued

38. "I'm not brave any more, darling. I'm all broken. They've broken me. I know it now." (Catherine, XLI)

39. That was what you did. You died. You did not know what it was about. You never had time to learn. They threw you in and told you the rules and the first time they caught you off base they killed you. Or they killed you gratuitously like Aymo. Or gave you the syphilis like Rinaldi. But they killed you in the end. You could count on that. Stay around and they would kill you. (XLI)

40. "Don't worry, darling. I'm not a bit afraid. It's just a dirty trick." (Catherine, XLI)

LESSON FIFTEEN

Objectives
1. To point out Hemingway's use of detail and dialogue to create and develop his themes
2. To further discuss and review *A Farewell To Arms*

Activity #1

Distribute the Quotations Worksheet. Read the first quotation aloud and ask students to locate it in their books. (The quotations on the list are given in the order in which they appear in the book. This quote is the opening sentence of Chapter 1.) Encourage students to offer their ideas about how the details in the quotation help them visualize the setting of the novel.

Next skip down to quotation 5 and ask a volunteer to read it aloud. Tell students that Passini says this in Chapter 9 when he and Lt. Henry are talking about war. Ask them to locate it in their books. Discuss how the use of dialogue helps the reader get a sense of the characters as well as understand the themes the author is presenting.

Continue discussing the quotations, either in order or randomly as you choose.

NOTE: This could also be done as an individual assignment in which students write down their own ideas about the significance of one or more quotations and then share their ideas orally with the whole group.

Activity #2

As an extension, have students find one or two additional quotations that they think are significant. Put a large piece of paper on a section of the blackboard or wall. Allow students to write their quotation on the paper, along with who said it and the page in the book where it is found. Leave the display of quotations available for students to read.

LESSON SIXTEEN

Objectives
1. To help students compile and organize the ideas presented in *A Farewell To Arms*
2. To give students the opportunity to practice their writing skills
3. To give the teacher the opportunity to evaluate students' writing skills and assess students' absorption of the materials covered in this unit

Activity
Distribute Writing Assignment #3 and discuss the directions in detail. Allow students ample time to complete the assignment.

LESSON SEVENTEEN

Objective
To review all of the vocabulary work done in this unit.

Activity
Choose one (or a few) of the vocabulary review games and activities listed on the pages which follow, and spend the class time doing this activity/these activities to review the vocabulary presented in the unit.

LESSON EIGHTEEN

Objective
To review the main events and ideas of *A Farewell To Arms*

Activity #1
Choose one of the review games/activities included in this packet and spend your class time as outlined there.

Activity #2
Remind students of the date of the unit test. Stress the review of the study guides and their class notes as a last minute, brush-up review.

WRITING ASSIGNMENT #3 *A Farewell To Arms*

PROMPT

We have discussed many aspects of *A Farewell To Arms*. The purpose of this assignment is to help you put all of those ideas into some order, some perspective. This writing assignment is in lieu of the essay portion of your unit test, a "take home" essay question which will be due at the end of the class period on the day of your unit test.

Your assignment is to answer the following question: What is the point of *A Farewell to Arms*, and how does Hemingway use the characters and events in the story to convey that message?

PREWRITING

Feel free to use all of your study guides, notes and the text. Your paper will be graded on the content, organization, your use of the English language, and appearance. You may want to make two columns on a piece of paper. In the left column list the characters and main events. Across from each item on the list make notes about how that character or event conveys the message.

You may also wish to do some outside reading on the topic. If you do, remember to use reputable sources.

DRAFTING

Start with an introductory paragraph that states the point or message of the novel. Then use an additional paragraph for each character or main event and explain how they convey the message. Use quotes or other details from the novel to support your ideas. You may also use quotes or summaries from other sources, but remember to cite these if they are used.

PEER CONFERENCEING/REVISING

When you finish the rough draft of your paper, ask another student to read it. After reading your rough draft, the student should tell you what he/she liked best about your work, which parts were difficult to understand, and ways in which your work could be improved. Reread your text considering your reviewer's comments. Make any revisions you think are necessary.

PROOFREADING/EDITING

Do a final proofreading of your paper, double-checking your grammar, spelling, organization, and the clarity of your ideas.

FINAL DRAFT

Follow your teacher's guidelines for completing the final draft of your paper.

VOCABULARY REVIEW ACTIVITIES
A Farewell To Arms

1. Divide your class into two teams and have an old-fashioned spelling or definition bee.

2. Give individuals or groups of students a *A Farewell to Arms* Vocabulary Word Search Puzzle with a word list. The person (group) to find all of the vocabulary words in the puzzle first wins.

3. Give students a *A Farewell to Arms* Vocabulary Word Search Puzzle without the word list. The person or group to find the most vocabulary words in the puzzle wins.

4. Put a *A Farewell to Arms* Vocabulary Crossword Puzzle onto a transparency on the overhead projector and do the puzzle together as a class.

5. Give students a *A Farewell to Arms* Vocabulary Matching Worksheet to do.

6. Use words from the word jumble page and have students spell them correctly, then use them in original sentences.

7. Have students write a story in which they correctly use as many vocabulary words as possible. Have students read their compositions orally. Post the most original compositions on your bulletin board.

8. Have students work in teams and play charades with the vocabulary words.

9. Select a word of the day and encourage students to use it correctly in their writing and speaking vocabulary.

10. Have a contest to see which students can find the most vocabulary words used in other sources. You may want to have a bulletin board available so the students can write down their word, the sentence it was used in, and the source.

11. Assign a word to each student, or let them choose a word. Have them look up the origin of the word, the part of speech, definition, a synonym, and an antonym. Then have them write a sentence using the word. Have students present their information orally to the class.

UNIT REVIEW GAMES/ACTIVITIES
A Farewell to Arms

1. Ask the class to make up a unit test for *A Farewell To Arms* (including a separate answer key). The test should have 4 sections: multiple choice, true/false, short answer, and essay. Students may use 1/2 period to make the test with a separate answer key and then swap papers and use the other 1/2 class period to take a test a classmate has devised. (open book) You may want to use the unit test included in this packet or take questions from the students' unit tests to formulate your own test.

2. Take 1/2 period for students to make up true and false questions (including the answers). Collect the papers, and divide the class into two teams. Draw a big tic-tac-toe board on the chalkboard. Make one team X and one team O. Ask questions to each side, giving each student one turn. If the question is answered correctly, that students' team's letter (X or O) is placed in the box. If the answer is incorrect, no mark is placed in the box. The object is to get three marks in a row like tic-tac-toe. You may want to keep track of the number of games won for each team.

3. Take 1/2 period for students to make up questions (true/false and short answer). Collect the questions. Divide the class into two teams. You'll alternate asking questions to individual members of teams A & B (like in a spelling bee). The question keeps going from A to B until it is correctly answered, then a new question is asked. A correct answer does not allow the team to get another question. Correct answers are +2 points; incorrect answers are -1 point.

4. Allow students time to quiz each other (in pairs or small groups) from their study guides and class notes.

5. Give students a *A Farewell to Arms* crossword puzzle to complete.

6. Divide your class into two teams. Use the *A Farewell to Arms* crossword words with their letters jumbled as a word list. Student 1 from Team A faces off against Student 1 from Team B. You write the first jumbled word on the board. The first student (1A or 1B) to unscramble the word wins the chance for his/her team to score points. If 1A wins the jumble, go to student 2A and give him/her a clue. He/she must give you the correct word which matches that clue. If he/she does, Team A scores a point, and you give student 3A a clue for which you expect another correct response. Continue giving Team A clues until some team member makes an incorrect response. An incorrect response sends the game back to the jumbled-word face off, this time with students 2A and 2B. Instead of repeating giving clues to the first few students of each team, continue with the student after the one who gave the last incorrect response on the team.

7. Take on the persona of "The Answer Person." Allow students to ask any question about the book. Answer the questions, or tell students where to look in the book to find the answer.

REVIEW GAMES/ACTIVITIES *A Farewell to Arms* Continued

8. Students may enjoy playing charades with events from the story. Select a student to start. Give him/her a card with a scene or event from the story. Allow the players to use their books to find the scene being described. The first person to guess each charade performs the next one.

9. Play a categories-type quiz game. (A master is included in this Unit Plan). Make an overhead transparency of the categories form. Divide the class into teams of three or four players each. Have each team choose a recorder and a banker. Choose a team to go first. That team will choose a category and point amount. Ask the question to the entire class.(Use the Study Guide Quiz and Vocabulary questions.) Give the teams one minute to discuss the answer and write it down. Walk around the room and check the answers. Each team that answers correctly receives the points. (Incorrect answers are not penalized; they just don't receive any points). Cross out that square on the playing board. Play continues until all squares have been used. The winning team is the one with the most points. You can assign bonus points to any square or squares you choose.

10. Have individual students draw scenes from the book. Display the scenes and have the rest of the class look in their books to find the chapter or section that is being depicted. The first student to find the correct scene then displays his or her picture. When the game is over, collect the pictures and put them in a binder for students to look at during their free time.

NOTE: If students do not need the extra review, omit this lesson and go on to the test.

LESSON NINETEEN

Objective
To test the students understanding of the main ideas, themes, and events in *A Farewell To Arms*

Activity #1
Distribute *A Farewell To Arms* tests. Discuss the directions in detail and allow students the entire class period to complete the test. If they finish this segment early, they may continue to work on their "take home" essays (Writing Assignment #3) until the end of the period.

Activity #2
Collect all test papers and assigned books prior to the end of the period.

NOTES ABOUT THE UNIT TESTS IN THIS UNIT:

There are 5 different unit tests which follow.

There are two short answer tests which are based primarily on facts from the novel. The answer key for short answer unit test 1 follows the student test. The answer key for short answer test 2 follows the student short answer unit test 2.

There is one advanced short answer unit test. It is based on the extra discussion questions. Use the matching key for short answer unit test 2 to check the matching section of the advanced short answer unit test. There is no key for the short answer questions. The answers will be based on the discussions you have had during class.

There are two multiple choice unit tests. Following the two unit tests, you will find an answer sheet on which students should mark their answers. The same answer sheet should be used for both tests; however, students' answers will be different for each test. Following the students' answer sheet for the multiple choice tests you will find your two keys: one for multiple-choice test 1 and one for multiple choice test 2. If you follow the directions at the top of each of those pages, you should be able to overlay your answer key on the students' answer sheets and easily grade the papers.

The short answer tests have a vocabulary section. You should choose 10 of the vocabulary words from this unit, read them orally and have the students write them down. Then, either have students write a definition or use the words in sentences. The second part of the vocabulary test is matching.

LESSON TWENTY

Objectives
    1. To widen the breadth of students' knowledge about the topics discussed or touched upon in *A Farewell to Arms*
    2. To present the nonfiction assignments

Activity #1
    Ask each student to give a brief oral report about the nonfiction work he/she read for the nonfiction assignment. Your criteria for evaluating this report will vary depending on the level of your students. You may wish for students to give the complete report without using notes of any kind. Or you may want students to read directly from a written report. You may want to do something between these two options. Make students aware of your criteria in ample time for them to prepare their reports.
    Start with one student's report. After that, ask if anyone else in the class has read on a topic related to the first student's report. If no one has, choose another student at random. After each report, be sure to ask if anyone has a report related to the one just completed. That will help keep continuity during the discussion of the reports.

Activity #2
    Collect the students' written reports. Put them in a binder and have the binder available for students to read.

Activity #3
    If the class or school has a Web site, post the nonfiction reports there.

UNIT TESTS

SHORT ANSWER UNIT TEST 1 *A Farewell to Arms*

I. Matching/Identification:
Directions: Match the term and its meaning.

____ 1. Rinaldi   A. supervisor of the hospital where Frederick was sent
____ 2. Ferguson   B. Frederick respected and share talks with this person
____ 3. Miss Van Campen C. a surgeon in Frederick's unit.
____ 4. Ettore   D. fixed Frederick's knee
____ 5. Simmons   E. a nurse who became Frederick's friend
____ 6. Dr. Valenti   F. Frederick's elderly billiards partner
____ 7. Piani   G. a "legitimate hero"; proud of rank and medals
____ 8. priest   H. ambulance driver for Frederick
____ 9. Miss Gage   I. a nurse and Catherine's friend
____ 10. Count Greffi   J. singer who befriended Frederick

II. Short Answer
Directions: Answer each question.

1. Identify the setting (time and place) and the narrator of the story.

2. Describe Frederick Henry's relationship to Catherine in these first few chapters.

Short Answer Unit Test 1 *A Farewell to Arms*

3. Under what circumstances was Lt. Henry wounded? Where was Lt. Henry wounded?

4. Why did Catherine take three nights off of night duty?

5. In Book II, what does Catherine do when she and Frederick part?

6. How do Frederick Henry, Bonello, Piani, and Aymo get separated from the rest of their unit?

Short Answer Unit Test 1 *A Farewell to Arms*

7. Why did Lt. Henry shoot the sergeant?

8. Why did Frederick Henry jump into the river? What could his jumping into the river signify?

9. How do Frederick and Catherine escape to Switzerland?

10. What went wrong with Catherine's delivery? How did Catherine die?

Short Answer Unit Test 1 *A Farewell to Arms*

III. Quotations
Directions: Identify the speaker and discuss the significance of each of the following quotations.

1. In the late summer of that year we lived in a house in a village that looked across the river and the plain to the mountain.

2. "There is a class that controls a country that is stupid and does not realize anything and never can. That is why we have this war."

3. I have noticed that doctors who fail in the practice of medicine have a tendency to seek one another's company and aid in consultation.

4. "I'll have to go back to the front pretty soon."
   "We won't think about that until you go."

5. But life isn't hard to manage when you've nothing to lose.

Short Answer Unit Test 1 *A Farewell to Arms*

III. Quotations, continued

6. "I am very tired of this war. If I was away I do not believe I would come back."

7. Abstract words such as glory, honor, courage or hallow were obscene beside the concrete names of villages, the numbers of roads, the names of rivers, the numbers of regiments and the dates.

8. The brave dies perhaps two thousand deaths if he's intelligent. He simply doesn't mention them.

9. "I never felt like a whore before . . . . I'm a good girl again . . . . I wish we could do something really sinful. Everything we do seems so innocent and simple. I can't believe we do anything wrong."

10. " . . . I can keep you safe. I know I can. But nobody can help themselves."

Short Answer Unit Test 1 *A Farewell to Arms*

IV: Essay

Are the characters in *A Farewell To Arms* stereotypes? If so, explain the usefulness of employing stereotypes in *A Farewell To Arms*. If they are not, explain how they merit individuality.

Short Answer Unit Test 1 *A Farewell to Arms*

V. Vocabulary Part 1
　　Listen to the vocabulary word and spell it. After you have spelled all the words, go back and write down the definitions.

WORD	DEFINITION
1. _____	_____
2. _____	_____
3. _____	_____
4. _____	_____
5. _____	_____
6. _____	_____
7. _____	_____
8. _____	_____
9. _____	_____
10. _____	_____

Vocabulary Part 2: Place the letter of the matching definition on the blank line.

_____　1. artillery　　　　A. leaves a dangerous place
_____　2. infantry　　　　B. argued
_____　3. conscientiously　C. bossy or controlling
_____　4. squabbled　　　 D. clumsy; not graceful
_____　5. evacuates　　　 E. large guns and cannons
_____　6. pry　　　　　　F. carefully
_____　7. intern　　　　　G. tense
_____　8. ungainly　　　　H. put in prison
_____　9. taut　　　　　　I. soldiers who fight on foot
_____　10. domineering　　J. force open

ANSWER KEY SHORT ANSWER UNIT TEST 1 *A Farewell to Arms*

I. Matching/Identification:

C 1. Rinaldi   A. supervisor of the hospital where Frederick was sent
I 2. Ferguson   B. Frederick respected and share talks with this person
A 3. Miss Van Campen   C. a surgeon in Frederick's unit
G 4. Ettore   D. fixed Frederick's knee
J 5. Simmons   E. a nurse who became Frederick's friend
D 6. Dr. Valenti   F. Frederick's elderly billiards partner
H 7. Piani   G. a "legitimate hero"; proud of rank and medals
B 8. priest   H. ambulance driver for Frederick
E 9. Miss Gage   I. a nurse and Catherine's friend
F 10. Count Greffi   J. singer who befriended Frederick

II. Short Answer

1. Identify the setting (time and place) and the narrator of the story.
     Most of the story takes place in Italy during World War I. The last book of the story takes place in Switzerland. Frederick Henry is the narrator. He is an American who has joined up with the Italian ambulance corps.

2. Describe Frederick Henry's relationship to Catherine in these first few chapters.
     Frederick Henry likes Catherine but is not in love with her and has no intentions of falling in love with her. He likes her but sees their relationship as a game in which one says and does what is expected whether it is meant or not.

3. Under what circumstances was Lt. Henry wounded? Where was Lt. Henry wounded?
     He was eating macaroni and cheese and drinking wine in a dugout which was hit by a trench mortar shell. He was wounded in the legs -- particularly his knee.

4. Why did Catherine take three nights off of night duty?
     She took three nights off to help to keep from arousing suspicions about her affair with Frederick Henry.

5. In Book II, what does Catherine do when she and Frederick part?
     Frederic says goodbye and gets into the carriage. Catherine smiles and waves to him.

6. How do Frederick Henry, Bonello, Piani, and Aymo get separated from the rest of their unit?
     They had helped to evacuate the rest of their post for the retreat and were to bring the "junk they've left" to Pordenone after tending to their vehicles. They are so tired they decide to get a little sleep before beginning their trip.

7. Why did Lt. Henry shoot the sergeant?

The sergeant would not obey the order to help push the cars out of the mud. The sergeants showed no respect for order or discipline.

8. Why did Frederick Henry jump into the river? What could his jumping into the river signify?

The battle police were questioning officers and killing them. He feared for his life and escaped into the river. It could signify his farewell to arms, his washing himself of the whole war, which has degenerated into total chaos. There is nothing he values left in the war; he moves on to a new stage in his life.

9. How do Frederick and Catherine escape to Switzerland?

The barman gives them a boat and food. They row the boat across the water to Switzerland.

10. What went wrong with Catherine's delivery? How did Catherine die?

The baby wouldn't come; she had to have a Caesarean delivery. The baby was choked by the cord and born dead. She had hemorrhages after the Caesarean operation.

III. Quotations

1. In the late summer of that year we lived in a house in a village that looked across the river and the plain to the mountain.

    This is the opening sentence of the novel. It describes the setting. (I)

2. "There is a class that controls a country that is stupid and does not realize anything and never can. That is why we have this war."

    Frederick says this. He is having a discussion about war with Passini. (IX)

3. I have noticed that doctors who fail in the practice of medicine have a tendency to seek one another's company and aid in consultation.

    This is Frederick's comment about the doctors who come to look at his knee. (XV)

4. "I'll have to go back to the front pretty soon."
   "We won't think about that until you go."

    Frederick and Catherine are talking. He is still convalescing but knows that he will soon have to go back to the war. (XVIII)

5. "But life isn't hard to manage when you've nothing to lose."

    Catherine says this to Frederick. He has just told her that he received papers for a leave. (XXI)

6. "I am very tired of this war. If I was away I do not believe I would come back."

    Signor Maggiore says this to Frederick when Frederick comes back into the town. (XXV)

7. Abstract words such as glory, honor, courage or hallow were obscene beside the concrete names of villages, the numbers of roads, the names of rivers, the numbers of regiments and the dates.
    Frederick as narrator says this when he is discussing war with some of the other soldiers. (XXVII)

8. The brave dies perhaps two thousand deaths if he's intelligent. He simply doesn't mention them.
    Catherine says this to Frederick. She has just told him that she is pregnant, and they are discussing love and bravery. (XXI)

9. "I never felt like a whore before . . .. I'm a good girl again . . .. I wish we could do something really sinful. Everything we do seems so innocent and simple. I can't believe we do anything wrong."
    Catherine says this to Frederick. They are in a hotel room on the night that he is about to return to the front. (XXIII)

10. " . . . I can keep you safe. I know I can. But nobody can help themselves."
    Catherine says this to Frederick. It is raining and she is telling him that she is afraid of the rain. (XIX)

V. Vocabulary Part 1
    Write in the words and definitions you have chosen to use for the test, if you wish..

Vocabulary Part 2:

E	1. artillery	A. leaves a dangerous place
I	2. infantry	B. argued
F	3. conscientiously	C. bossy or controlling
B	4. squabbled	D. clumsy; not graceful
A	5. evacuates	E. large guns and cannons
J	6. pry	F. carefully
H	7. intern	G. tense
D	8. ungainly	H. put in prison
G	9. taut	I. soldiers who fight on foot
C	10. domineering	J. force open

SHORT ANSWER UNIT TEST 2 A Farewell to Arms

I. Matching/Identification:
Directions: Match the term and its meaning.

_____ 1. Aymo	A. surgeon who lived the pleasures of life
_____ 2. Mrs. Walker	B. nurse and Catherine's friend
_____ 3. Simmons	C. a true "Hemingway man"
_____ 4. Rinaldi	D. helped Frederick escape
_____ 5. Ettore	E. cheated at races
_____ 6. Ferguson	F. ambulance driver who got shot on the way to Pordenone
_____ 7. Dr. Valenti	G. nurse and Frederick's friend
_____ 8. barman	H. did not share values with Frederick and Catherine
_____ 9. Myers	I. singer who befriended Frederick
_____ 10. Miss Gage	J. first "useless" nurse Frederick encountered

II. Short Answer

1. Who is the narrator? What is his position?

2. The priest is introduced in the first few chapters. What is his relationship with Frederick Henry? Rinaldi?

Short Answer Unit Test 2 *A Farewell to Arms*

3. What kind of a woman is Catherine Barkley?

4. In Chapter 7, what is the point of the incident with the soldier who had a rupture?

5. Why does Frederick Henry want to marry Catherine? What is her response?

6. Why didn't Frederick go on convalescent leave?

Short Answer Unit Test 2 *A Farewell to Arms*

7. Frederick Henry says, "I was always embarrassed by the words sacred, glorious, and sacrifice and the expression in vain." Why did he feel that way?

8. Why did Frederick Henry jump into the river? What could his jumping into the river signify?

9. Where did Frederick Henry meet up with Catherine after he escapes from the river?

10. What happened to Catherine at the end of the story?

Short Answer Unit Test 2 *A Farewell to Arms*

III. Quotations
Directions: Identify the speaker and discuss the significance of each of the following quotations.

1. He was a legitimate hero who bored everyone he met. Catherine could not stand him.

2. ". . . there's only us two and in the world there's all the rest of them. If anything comes between us we're gone and then they have us."

3. "You see we don't believe in the war anyway, Tenente."

4. "I'm afraid of the rain because sometimes I see me dead in it."

5. This was a game, like bridge, in which you said things instead of playing cards. Nobody had mentioned what the stakes were. It was alright with me.

Short Answer Unit Test 2 *A Farewell to Arms*

6. "You rank as an officer. I am an officer."
   "I am not really. You are not even an Italian. You are a foreigner."
   "You should be respected."

7. He had a rotten life in the mess and he was fine about it but I thought how he would be in his own country.

8. "We think. We read. We are not peasants. We are mechanics. But even the peasants know better than to believe in a war. Everybody hates this war."

9. "You'll die then. Fight or die. That's what people do. They don't marry."

10. "I'm not brave any more, darling. I'm all broken. They've broken me. I know it now."

Short Answer Unit Test 2 *A Farewell to Arms*

IV: Essay
Plot and describe Frederick's growth as a character through the novel.

Short Answer Unit Test 2 *A Farewell to Arms*

V. Vocabulary Part 1
　　Listen to the vocabulary word and spell it. After you have spelled all the words, go back and write down the definitions.

	WORD	DEFINITION
1.	_____	_____
2.	_____	_____
3.	_____	_____
4.	_____	_____
5.	_____	_____
6.	_____	_____
7.	_____	_____
8.	_____	_____
9.	_____	_____
10.	_____	_____

V. Vocabulary Part II
Directions: Place the letter of the matching definition on the blank line.

_____ 1. groggy　　　　A. causes water to flow or drop off
_____ 2. sheds　　　　 B. examining carefully
_____ 3. chalet　　　　C. protesters
_____ 4. torrent　　　　D. morally offensive
_____ 5. agitators　　　E. weak or dizzy
_____ 6. vague　　　　 F. official document of praise
_____ 7. scrutinizing　　G. fast, powerful flood of water
_____ 8. obscene　　　 H. route; path
_____ 9. trajectory　　　I. traditional Swiss wooden cottage
_____ 10. citation　　　 J. not clear in meaning

ANSWER KEY SHORT ANSWER UNIT TEST 2 *A Farewell to Arms*

I. Matching/Identification:

F 1. Aymo   A. surgeon who lived the pleasures of life
J 2. Mrs. Walker   B. nurse and Catherine's friend
I 3. Simmons   C. a true "Hemingway man"
A 4. Rinaldi   D. helped Frederick escape
H 5. Ettore   E. cheated at races
B 6. Ferguson   F. ambulance driver who got shot on the way to Pordenone
C 7. Dr. Valenti   G. nurse and Frederick's friend
D 8. barman   H. did not share values with Frederick and Catherine
E 9. Myers   I. singer who befriended Frederick
G 10. Miss Gage   J. first "useless" nurse Frederick encountered

II. Short Answer

1. Who is the narrator? What is his position?
    Frederick Henry is the narrator. He is an American who has joined up with the Italian ambulance core.

2. The priest is introduced in the first few chapters. What is his relationship with Frederick Henry? Rinaldi?
    He is the object of Rinaldi's teasing and jokes. Frederick Henry doesn't join in the "baiting" of the priest; he gives the priest some respect.

3. What kind of a woman is Catherine Barkley?
    Catherine's fiancé was killed in the war. She is a bit vulnerable and "a little crazy" at the time she meets Frederick Henry. She likes him, realizes that their relationship is "a rotten game" and is willing to be involved anyway.

4. In Chapter 7, what is the point of the incident with the soldier who had a rupture?
    It shows the general negative attitude towards the war.

5. Why does Frederick Henry want to marry Catherine? What is her response?
    He thinks they should get married. He has concerns about the possibilities of their having a child or his being killed. Also, he doesn't want her to leave him. She considers them already married. "It would mean everything to me if I had any religion. But I haven't any religion."

6. Why didn't Frederick go on convalescent leave?
    He got jaundice, his drinking was discovered, and he lost his leave.

7. Frederick Henry says, "I was always embarrassed by the words sacred, glorious, and sacrifice and the expression in vain." Why did he feel that way?

    Frederick is a man of action, a man who understands and values concrete reality. Abstract words don't mean anything; the actions which cause the words to be used are important -- the words alone are not.

8. Why did Frederick Henry jump into the river? What could his jumping into the river signify?

    The battle police were questioning officers and killing them. He feared for his life and escaped into the river. It could signify his farewell to arms, his washing himself of the whole war, which has degenerated into total chaos. There is nothing he values left in the war; he moves on to a new stage in his life.

9. Where did Frederick Henry meet up with Catherine after he escapes from the river?

    He finds her at Stresa.

10. What happened to Catherine at the end of the story?

    The baby wouldn't come; she had to have a Caesarean delivery. The baby was choked by the cord and born dead. Catherine had hemorrhages after the Caesarean operation, and died.

III. Quotations

1. He was a legitimate hero who bored everyone he met. Catherine could not stand him.

    Frederick is talking about Ettore, one of the Italian soldiers. (XIX)

2. ". . . there's only us two and in the world there's all the rest of them. If anything comes between us we're gone and then they have us."

    Catherine is talking to Frederick. She has just told him that she is pregnant. They have had a small misunderstanding and she wants to make sure they don't have another one. (XXI)

3. "You see we don't believe in the war anyway, Tenente."

    Piani says this to Frederick. They are in a hayloft, having just escaped from the Germans and then a group of Italian soldiers who were shooting everyone, thinking they were Germans in Italian uniforms. (XXX)

4. "I'm afraid of the rain because sometimes I see me dead in it."

    Catherine tells this to Frederick. (XIX)

5. This was a game, like bridge, in which you said things instead of playing cards. Nobody had mentioned what the stakes were. It was alright with me.

    Frederick as narrator says this about Catherine early in their relationship. (VI)

6. "You rank as an officer. I am an officer." (Frederick to priest)
"I am not really. You are not even an Italian. You are a foreigner." (priest to Frederick)
"You should be respected."(Frederick to priest) (XI)
    This is a conversation between Frederick and the priest. They are talking about the other men and the war. (XI)

7. He had a rotten life in the mess and he was fine about it but I thought how he would be in his own country.
    Frederick as narrator says this about the priest. The priest has just left after a visit with Frederick. (XI)

8. "We think. We read. We are not peasants. We are mechanics. But even the peasants know better than to believe in a war. Everybody hates this war."
    Passini says this to Frederick and the other members of the ambulance corps during a conversation about the war. (IX)

9. "You'll die then. Fight or die. That's what people do. They don't marry."
    Miss Ferguson says this to Frederick Henry. Frederick had asked Miss Ferguson if she would come to his and Catherine's wedding. Miss Ferguson replied that she did not think they would ever get married. (XVI)

10. "I'm not brave any more, darling. I'm all broken. They've broken me. I know it now."
    Catherine says this to Frederick. She is in labor and is having a difficult time. (XLI)

V. Vocabulary Part 1
    Write in the words and definitions you have chosen, if you wish.

V. Vocabulary Part II

E	1. groggy	A. causes water to flow or drop off
A	2. sheds	B. examining carefully
I	3. chalet	C. protesters
G	4. torrent	D. morally offensive
C	5. agitators	E. weak or dizzy
J	6. vague	F. official document of praise
B	7. scrutinizing	G. fast, powerful flood of water
D	8. obscene	H. route; path
H	9. trajectory	I. traditional Swiss wooden cottage
F	10. citation	J. not clear in meaning

MULTIPLE CHOICE UNIT TEST 1 *A Farewell to Arms*

I. Matching/Identification:
1. Rinaldi
2. Ferguson
3. Miss Van Campen
4. Ettore
5. Simmons
6. Dr. Valenti
7. Piani
8. priest
9. Miss Gage
10. Count Greffi

A. supervisor of the hospital where Frederick was sent
B. Frederick respected and share talks with this person
C. a surgeon in Frederick's uniT
D. fixed Frederick's knee
E. a nurse who became Frederick's friend
F. Frederick's elderly billiards partner
G. a "legitimate hero"; proud of rank and medals
H. ambulance driver for Frederick
I. a nurse and Catherine's friend
J. singer who befriended Frederick

II. Multiple Choice
1. Where and when does the story take place?
   A. in France during World War II
   B. in Italy during World War I
   C. in Germany between the two world wars
   D. in modern-day Switzerland

2. True or False: In the first few chapters of Book I, Frederick Henry is madly in love with Catherine.
   A. True
   B. False

3. Where was Lt. Henry wounded?
   A. He was wounded in the legs, especially the knees.
   B. He was wounded in the head and chest.
   C. He was wounded in the back.
   D. He was wounded in the arms and shoulders.

4. What did Catherine do to help keep from arousing suspicions about her affair with Frederick Henry?
   A. She started wearing an engagement ring.
   B. She stopped speaking to Frederick.
   C. She took three nights off.
   D. She transferred to a different hospital.

Multiple Choice Unit Test 1 *A Farewell to Arms*

5. In Book II, what does Catherine do when she and Frederick part?
    A. She cries hysterically.
    B. She turns her back and walks away.
    C. She blows him a kiss.
    D. She smiles and waves.

6. How do Frederick Henry, Bonello, Piani, and Aymo get separated from the rest of their unit?
    A. They are tired and fall asleep.
    B. Their truck gets a flat tire.
    C. They stop to make dinner.
    D. They make a wrong turn and get lost.

7. What did Lt. Henry do to the sergeant because the sergeant did not show respect for the order of discipline and help push the cars out of the mud?
    A. He demoted him to private.
    B. He shot him.
    C. He sent him to jail.
    D. He slapped him.

8. What did Frederick Henry do when the police were questioning officers and killing them?
    A. He fell down and played dead until they left.
    B. He grabbed a rifle and shot all of them.
    C. He jumped into the river and escaped.
    D. He got in the truck and drove through them.

9. How do Frederick and Catherine escape to Switzerland?
    A. The barman gives them a boat and food.
    B. The hotel owner smuggles them in a wagon.
    C. They boldly take a train and act normal.
    D. They use false papers and walk across the border.

10. True or False: The delivery of the baby goes well and a healthy girl is born.
    A. True
    B. False

Multiple Choice Unit Test 1 *A Farewell to Arms*

III. Quotations
Directions: Match the two parts of each quotation.

1. In the late summer of that year we lived in a house in a village ____

2. "There is a class that controls a country that is stupid and does not realize anything and never can. ____

3. I have noticed that doctors who fail in the practice of medicine ____

4. "I'll have to go back to the front pretty soon." ____

5. "But life isn't hard to manage ____

6. "I am very tired of this war. ____

7. Abstract words such as glory, honor, courage, or hallow were obscene ____

8. "The brave dies perhaps two thousand deaths if he's intelligent ____

9. "I never felt like a whore before . . . I'm a good girl again . . . ____

10. "I can keep you safe. I know I can. ____

A. "We won't think about that until you go."
B. beside the concrete names of villages, the numbers of roads, the names of rivers, the numbers of regiments, and the dates.
C. But nobody can help themselves."
D. If I was away I do not believe I would come back."
E. That is why we have this war."
F. I wish we could do something really sinful. Everything we do seems so innocent and simple. I can't believe we do anything wrong."
G. that looked across the river and the plain to the mountain.
H. He simply doesn't mention them."
I. have a tendency to seek one another's company and aid in consultation.
J. when you've nothing to lose."

MULTIPLE CHOICE UNIT TEST 1 *A Farewell to Arms*

IV. Vocabulary Part I Directions: Match the word and its meaning.

1. artillery
2. infantry
3. conscientiously
4. squabbled
5. evacuates
6. pry
7. intern
8. ungainly
9. taut
10. domineering

A. leaves a dangerous place
B. argued
C. bossy or controlling
D. clumsy; not graceful
E. large guns and cannons
F. carefully
G. tense
H. put in prison
I. soldiers who fight on foot
J. force open

Vocabulary Part 2 Directions: Mark the letter next to the word that matches the definition.

11. a disease of the intestines
    A. bile
    B. brittleness
    C. cholera
    D. tourniquet

12. started
    A. decorated
    B. commenced
    C. refrained
    D. elated

13. serious; humorless
    A. offensive
    B. legitimate
    C. unchaperoned
    D. solemn

14. thoughts based on feelings
    A. sentiment
    B. regiment
    C. projectile
    D. remorse

15. having a high opinion of self
    A. coagulates
    B. conceited
    C. articulation
    D. vague

16. people who do not believe in God
    A. anarchists
    B. socialists
    C. agitators
    D. atheists

17. loss of blood
    A. hemorrhage
    B. truss
    C. emery
    D. rucksack

18. in short supply; limited
    A. hostile
    B. scarce
    C. gyps
    D. fragments

19. in a disapproving way
    A. cordial
    B. bellows
    C. contemptuously
    D. camions

20. sarcasm; mocking
    A. cynicism
    B. trajectory
    C. groggy
    D. dormer

MULTIPLE CHOICE UNIT TEST 2 *A Farewell to Arms*

I. Matching/Identification:
Directions: Match the term and its meaning.

1. Aymo	A. surgeon who lived the pleasures of life
2. Mrs. Walker	B. nurse and Catherine's friend
3. Simmons	C. a true "Hemingway man"
4. Rinaldi	D. helped Frederick escape
5. Ettore	E. cheated at races
6. Ferguson	F. ambulance driver who got shot on the way to Pordenone
7. Dr. Valenti	G. nurse and Frederick's friend
8. barman	H. did not share values with Frederick and Catherine
9. Myers	I. singer who befriended Frederick
10. Miss Gage	J. first "useless" nurse Frederick encountered

II. Multiple Choice

1. Frederick Henry is the narrator of the story. What is his position?
   A. He is a German journalist stationed in Italy.
   B. He is the ambassador to Spain.
   C. He is a French resistance fighter.
   D. He is an American who has joined up with the Italian ambulance corps.

2. Who is the object of Rinaldi's teasing and jokes?
   A. the lieutenant
   B. the priest
   C. the chief surgeon
   D. the cook

3. True or False: Catherine Barkley realizes her relationship with Frederick Henry is "a rotten game" but is willing to be involved anyway.
   A. True
   B. False

4. In Chapter 7, what is the point of the incident with the soldier who had a rupture?
   A. It shows man's inhumanity to man.
   B. It shows the sad state of medical technology.
   C. It shows the prejudice toward the lower ranks.
   D. It shows the general negative attitude towards the war.

Multiple Choice Unit Test 2 *A Farewell to Arms*

5. Frederick wants to marry Catherine. What is her response?
    A. She considers them already married.
    B. She says she will never marry.
    C. She says they have to get permission from the priest first.
    D. She says she will marry him if the Allies win the war.

6. Why didn't Frederick go on convalescent leave?
    A. There was nowhere safe to go.
    B. He got jaundice, his drinking was discovered, and he lost his leave.
    C. He did not want to go without Catherine and she could not go.
    D. He was not considered sick enough to get leave.

7. How did Frederick feel about the words *sacred, glorious, sacrifice,* and *in vain*?
    A. angry
    B. enthusiastic
    C. embarrassed
    D. apathetic

8. What action symbolized Frederick's farewell to arms and moving to a new stage of his life.
    A. jumping into the river
    B. saying he loved Catherine
    C. burning his uniform
    D. tearing up his military identification papers

9. Where did Catherine and Frederick go to play, walk, talk, and eat?
    A. to Spain
    B. to Switzerland
    C. to Monaco
    D. to Sweden

10. What happened to Catherine and the baby?
    A. She had the baby but refused to marry Frederick.
    B. She had the baby and went to America with Frederick.
    C. She lived but the baby died.
    D. The baby died. She had hemorrhages after the Caesarean operation and died.

Multiple Choice Unit Test 2 *A Farewell to Arms*

III. Quotations
Directions: Match the two parts of each quotation.

1. He was a legitimate hero who bored everyone he met. ____

2. ". . . there's only us two and in the world there's all the rest of them. ____

3. "You see we don't ___

4. "I'm afraid of the rain because ___

5. This was a game, like bridge, in which you said things instead of playing cards ___

6. "You rank as an officer. I am an officer." /"I am not really." ____

7. He had a rotten life in the mess and he was fine about it ____

8. "We think. We read. We are not peasants. We are mechanics. ___

9. "You'll die then. Fight or die. ___

10. "I'm not brave any more, darling. ___

A. believe in the war anyway, Tenente."
B. Nobody had mentioned what the stakes were. It was alright with me.
C. "You are not even an Italian. You are a foreigner."/ "You should be respected."
D. Catherine could not stand him.
E. But even the peasants know better than to believe in a war. Everybody hates this war."
F. That's what people do. They don't marry."
G. If anything comes between us we're gone and then they have us."
H. I'm all broken. They've broken me. I know it now."
I. but I thought how he would be in his own country.
J. sometimes I see me dead in it."

Multiple Choice Unit Test 2 *A Farewell to Arms*

IV. Vocabulary Part I Directions: Match the word and its meaning.

1. groggy   A. causes water to flow or drop off
2. sheds   B. examining carefully
3. chalet   C. protesters
4. torrent   D. morally offensive
5. agitators   E. weak or dizzy
6. vague   F. official document of praise
7. scrutinizing   G. fast, powerful flood of water
8. obscene   H. route; path
9. trajectory   I. traditional Swiss wooden cottage
10. citation   J. not clear in meaning

Vocabulary Part 2 Directions: Mark the letter next to the word that matches the definition.

11. not accompanied by a supervisor
    A. legitimate
    B. conceited
    C. impartially
    D. unchaperoned

12. strong feeling of guilt or sorrow
    A. sector
    B. remorse
    C. cynicism
    D. obstacles

13. reduce someone's confidence
    A. puncture
    B. scrutinizing
    C. evacuates
    D. articulation

14. very religious
    A. atheist
    B. scarce
    C. devout
    D. solemn

15. thickens into a soft mass
    A. coagulates
    B. camions
    C. obstacles
    D. gusts

16. showing hatred toward another
    A. bile
    B. hostile
    C. summarily
    D. exhilaration

17. cheats out of money
    A. pry
    B. squabbled
    C. gyps
    D. domineering

18. a window built at right angles to the roof
    A. intern
    B. dormer
    C. emery
    D. trajectory

29. a belief that is actually incorrect
    A. fallacy
    B. porter
    C. rucksack
    D. formalities

20. weak and likely to break or crack
    A. impartially
    B. conceited
    C. ungainly
    D. brittleness

ANSWER SHEET Multiple Choice Unit Tests 1, 2 *A Farewell to Arms*

I. Matching	III. Quotations	IV. Vocabulary
1.	1.	1.
2.	2.	2.
3.	3.	3.
4.	4.	4.
5.	5.	5.
6.	6.	6.
7.	7.	7.
8.	8.	8.
9.	9.	9.
10.	10.	10.
		11.
		12.
		13.
		14.
		15.
		16.
		17.
		18.
		19.
		20.

II. Multiple Choice

1. (A) (B) (C) (D)
2. (A) (B) (C) (D)
3. (A) (B) (C) (D)
4. (A) (B) (C) (D)
5. (A) (B) (C) (D)
6. (A) (B) (C) (D)
7. (A) (B) (C) (D)
8. (A) (B) (C) (D)
9. (A) (B) (C) (D)
10. (A) (B) (C) (D)

ANSWER SHEET KEY Multiple Choice Unit Test 1 *A Farewell to Arms*

I. Matching	III. Quotations	IV. Vocabulary
1. C	1. G	1. E
2. I	2. E	2. I
3. A	3. I	3. F
4. G	4. A	4. B
5. J	5. J	5. A
6. D	6. D	6. J
7. H	7. B	7. H
8. B	8. H	8. D
9. E	9. F	9. G
10. F	10. C	10. C
		11. C

II. Multiple Choice

1. (A) ( ) (C) (D)   12. B
2. (A) ( ) (C) (D)   13. D
3. ( ) (B) (C) (D)   14. A
4. (A) (B) ( ) (D)   15. B
5. (A) (B) (C) ( )   16. D
6. ( ) (B) (C) (D)   17. A
7. (A) ( ) (C) (D) 18. B
8. (A) (B) ( ) (D)   19. C
9. ( ) (B) (C) (D)   20. A
10. (A) ( ) (C) (D)

ANSWER SHEET KEY Multiple Choice Unit Test 2 *A Farewell to Arms*

I. Matching	III. Quotations	IV. Vocabulary
1. F	1. D	1. E
2. J	2. G	2. A
3. I	3. A	3. I
4. A	4. J	4. G
5. H	5. B	5. C
6. B	6. C	6. J
7. C	7. I	7. B
8. D	8. E	8. D
9. E	9. F	9. H
10. G	10. H	10. F
		11. D

II. Multiple Choice

1. (A) (B) (C) ( )
2. (A) ( ) (C) (D)
3. ( ) (B) (C) (D)
4. (A) (B) (C) ( )
5. ( ) (B) (C) (D)
6. (A) ( ) (C) (D)
7. (A) (B) ( ) (D)
8. ( ) (B) (C) (D)
9. (A) ( ) (C) (D)
10. (A) (B) (C) ( )

12. B
13. A
14. C
15. A
16. B
17. C
18. B
19. A
20. D

UNIT RESOURCE MATERIALS

EXTRA ACTIVITIES *Farewell To Arms*

One of the difficulties in teaching a novel is that all students don't read at the same speed. One student who likes to read may take the book home and finish it in a day or two. Sometimes a few students finish the in-class assignments early. The problem, then, is finding suitable extra activities for students.

One thing that helps is to keep a little library in the classroom. For this unit on *A Farewell To Arms*, you might check out from the school library other novels and stories by Hemingway. A biography or articles about the author would be interesting for some students. You can include other related books and articles about World War I, nursing, careers in medicine, Switzerland, Italy, winter sports, careers in the services, ambulance and rescue crews, or articles of criticism about Hemingway's works.

Other things you may keep on hand are puzzles and worksheets. We have made some for you. Feel free to duplicate them for your students.

Some students may like to draw. You might devise a contest or allow some extra-credit grade for students who draw characters or scenes from *A Farewell To Arms*. Note, too, that if the students do not want to keep their drawings you may pick up some extra bulletin board materials this way. If you have a contest and you supply the prize (a CD or something like that perhaps), you could, possibly, make the drawing itself a non-refundable entry fee.

BULLETIN BOARD IDEAS *A Farewell To Arms*

1. Save one corner of the board for the best of students' *A Farewell To Arms* writing assignments.

2. Take one of the word search puzzles from the extra activities packet and (with a marker) copy it over in a large size on the bulletin board. Write the clue words to one side. Invite students prior to and after class to find the words and circle them on the bulletin board.

3. Title the board "WAR BROTHERS" in cut-out letters. Put up a collage of scenes from magazines, the library or other sources showing soldiers, people helping others after a disaster, etc. (You may ask students to find pictures as an assignment and have each one put up his picture on the bulletin board).

4. Title the board *A Farewell To Arms* in cut-out letters and write various significant quotes from the novel (see the study guides or notes) on colored paper. Post the quotes on the board.

5. Title the board *A Farewell To Arms* in cut-out letters. Post pictures and facts briefly explaining the history of World War I, facts which will put Frederick Henry's involvement into a perspective.

6. Make a bulletin board about sentence structure. Take one of Hemingway's passages and label the parts of the sentences. Write the passage (on the bulletin board) as many ways as you can and label the parts to show the different sentence structures.

7. Put up a big map of Italy and Switzerland. Place big red stars on the locations mentioned in the novel.

8. Make a travel bulletin board for Italy and Switzerland, showing places to go and things to do there. (Your local travel agency may have some good materials for this board!)

9. Make a bulletin board relating to the armed services and the opportunities available there. (Your local recruiting offices will have loads of stuff for you!)

10. Title the board HEROES. Have each student think of a word which would describe a hero and find a picture showing that characteristic. Each student should mount his picture on a colorful sheet of paper and write his word in bold letters under (or next to) the picture. Post the pictures on the board.

MORE ACTIVITIES
A Farewell To Arms

1. Have students design a book cover (front and back and inside flaps) for *A Farewell To Arms*.

2. Have students design a bulletin board (ready to be put up; not just sketched) for *A Farewell To Arms*.

3. Have a guest speaker give background about World War I.

4. Use some of the related topics (noted earlier for an in-class library) as topics for research, reports or written papers, or as topics for guest speakers.

5. Research what careers are currently available in the armed services and medical professions.

6. Read aloud some of the parodies students have written of *A Farewell To Arms*.

7. Have students compare this story to another war story they have read or seen. (*Gone With The Wind, The Red Badge of Courage*, etc.)

A Farewell To Arms Unit Word Search

```
A E T T O R E V E L Y R N S R T P H P
N Z H H T L P G I E Z I B F I R R J V
T W G R X G A G V G A V A W N I E S F
H M I T Y G H W Q R V E R W A C G M M
O E F S J T S L W B K R K W L K N T N
N F N Q D E D N U O W B L M D P A T Y
Y B S R H O S P I T A L E E I K N L W
N F W G Y V M V Y D V Z Y C N L T P T
E G I R B F G L W I N I T N E L A V D
W W T B J C K L W V S Y S A H Y C N L
S D Z C D T C L X E I B R L F K C N C
P C E Z P S V V G H T D E U J R E B E
A M R F E E X A K C A B D B P P R F D
P W L K A I H T N F L K R M M O I G O
E N A C I R E M A U Y B O A T L N L V
R N N R R P E L L B R M C H V A L A H
S R D O E D P W A O Y S E P M E G D S
B M M A D S F B E A V R E R N X Z E R
D E C I D N U A J L S E A O M A R M S
H E A N G E R E E B L B B G R E F F I
```

ALPS	BONELLO	ITALY	PREGNANT
AMBULANCE	BRAVE	JAUNDICE	PRIEST
AMERICAN	BROTHERS	LEG	RAIN
ANGER	CAMPEN	LIFE	RINALDI
ANTHONY	ETTORE	LIGHT	RIVER
ARMS	FAREWELL	LOVE	SNAKE
AYMO	FIGHT	MEDAL	SWITZERLAND
BABY	GAGE	MILAN	TRICK
BARKLEY	GREFFI	NEWSPAPERS	VALENTINI
BARMAN	HEMORRHAGES	NURSE	WAR
BEER	HENRY	ORDERS	WISDOM
BOAT	HOSPITAL	PEACE	WOUNDED

A Farewell To Arms Unit Word Search Answer Key

ALPS	BONELLO	ITALY	PREGNANT
AMBULANCE	BRAVE	JAUNDICE	PRIEST
AMERICAN	BROTHERS	LEG	RAIN
ANGER	CAMPEN	LIFE	RINALDI
ANTHONY	ETTORE	LIGHT	RIVER
ARMS	FAREWELL	LOVE	SNAKE
AYMO	FIGHT	MEDAL	SWITZERLAND
BABY	GAGE	MILAN	TRICK
BARKLEY	GREFFI	NEWSPAPERS	VALENTINI
BARMAN	HEMORRHAGES	NURSE	WAR
BEER	HENRY	ORDERS	WISDOM
BOAT	HOSPITAL	PEACE	WOUNDED

A Farewell To Arms Crossword

Across
1. Frederick Henry joined this corps
7. I'm not a bit afraid. It's just a dirty ___.
9. ___ was washed away in the river along with any obligation.
11. It would help keep the baby small
12. A ___ person dies two thousand deaths but never mentions it
13. The barman gives Frederick & Catherine a ___ and food
16. In war, one side ____s the other
18. Narrator: Frederick _____
20. Place Frederick jumped into to escape
21. Place where sick & wounded people are treated
24. Award
26. I was going to forget the war. I had made a separate ___.
27. World ___ I
28. Name of the mountain range

Down
2. He helped Frederick and Catherine
3. Where Frederick was wounded
4. The priest brought Frederick vermouth and ___ in the hospital.
5. Catherine thinks he's boring
6. It was born dead
8. Place where story takes place
9. A Farewell to ___
10. Frederick played billiards with him
13. Catherine's last name
14. Frederick Henry's nationality
15. Feeling of Frederick towards Catherine
16. A ___ To Arms
17. Friend to Frederick and Catherine
19. Catherine is afraid of it
22. They must be obeyed
23. Was shot by mistake by Italians
25. But ___ isn't hard to manage when you've nothing to lose.

A Farewell To Arms Crossword Answer Key

						1 A	2 M	B	3 U	L	4 A	N	5 C	E		
	6 B								A		E		E		7 T	8 R	I	C	K
	A			9 A	N	10 G	E	R			G		W		T		T		
	11 B	E	E	R		R		M					S		O		A		
	Y			M		E		A		12 B	R	A	V	E			L		
13 B	O	14 A	T			F		N					P				Y		
A		M		15 L		16 F	I	17 G	H	T		18 H	E	N	19 R	Y	
R		E		O		A		A				R			A		
K		20 R	I	V	E	R		G		21 H	22 O	S	P	I	T	23 A	L
L		I		E		E		E			R				N		Y
E		C				W				24 M	E	D	25 A	L			M
Y		A			26 P	E	A	C	E				L				O
		N				L				27 W	A	R		F			
				28 A	L	P	S						S		E		

Across
1. Frederick Henry joined this corps
7. I'm not a bit afraid. It's just a dirty ___.
9. ___ was washed away in the river along with any obligation.
11. It would help keep the baby small
12. A ___ person dies two thousand deaths but never mentions it
13. The barman gives Frederick & Catherine a ___ and food
16. In war, one side ____s the other
18. Narrator: Frederick _____
20. Place Frederick jumped into to escape
21. Place where sick & wounded people are treated
24. Award
26. I was going to forget the war. I had made a separate ___.
27. World ___ I
28. Name of the mountain range

Down
2. He helped Frederick and Catherine
3. Where Frederick was wounded
4. The priest brought Frederick vermouth and ___ in the hospital.
5. Catherine thinks he's boring
6. It was born dead
8. Place where story takes place
9. A Farewell to ___
10. Frederick played billiards with him
13. Catherine's last name
14. Frederick Henry's nationality
15. Feeling of Frederick towards Catherine
16. A ___ To Arms
17. Friend to Frederick and Catherine
19. Catherine is afraid of it
22. They must be obeyed
23. Was shot by mistake by Italians
25. But ___ isn't hard to manage when you've nothing to lose.

MATCHING QUIZ/WORKSHEET 1 - A Farewell To Arms

___ 1. ITALY A. Catherine's last name

___ 2. WOUNDED B. Catherine is afraid of it

___ 3. BARMAN C. Dear boy, that's not ___. That is cynicism.

___ 4. AMBULANCE D. A Farewell to ___

___ 5. RAIN E. Narrator: Frederick _____

___ 6. ETTORE F. Frederick Henry joined this corps

___ 7. BABY G. Name of the mountain range

___ 8. ARMS H. It was born dead

___ 9. RIVER I. Catherine died having ___ after the operation

___ 10. GAGE J. In war, one side ____s the other

___ 11. HENRY K. The neutral country

___ 12. AYMO L. Feeling of Frederick towards Catherine

___ 13. ALPS M. Hospital supervisor; Van ____

___ 14. FIGHT N. Place Frederick jumped into to escape

___ 15. RINALDI O. Friend to Frederick and Catherine

___ 16. LOVE P. Place where story takes place

___ 17. BARKLEY Q. He helped Frederick and Catherine

___ 18. HEMORRHAGES R. Hurt but not killed

___ 19. AMERICAN S. He was going to marry Catherine before Frederick met her.

___ 20. CAMPEN T. Was shot by mistake by Italians

___ 21. SWITZERLAND U. Catherine thinks he's boring

___ 22. WISDOM V. Place where sick & wounded people are treated

___ 23. HEMINGWAY W. Hospital where Catherine was transferred

___ 24. HOSPITAL X. Author

___ 25. MILAN Y. Frederick Henry's nationality

KEY: MATCHING QUIZ/WORKSHEET 1 - A Farewell To Arms

P - 1.	ITALY	A. Catherine's last name
R - 2.	WOUNDED	B. Catherine is afraid of it
Q - 3.	BARMAN	C. Dear boy, that's not ___. That is cynicism.
F - 4.	AMBULANCE	D. A Farewell to ___
B - 5.	RAIN	E. Narrator: Frederick _____
U - 6.	ETTORE	F. Frederick Henry joined this corps
H - 7.	BABY	G. Name of the mountain range
D - 8.	ARMS	H. It was born dead
N - 9.	RIVER	I. Catherine died having ___ after the operation
O - 10.	GAGE	J. In war, one side ____s the other
E - 11.	HENRY	K. The neutral country
T - 12.	AYMO	L. Feeling of Frederick towards Catherine
G - 13.	ALPS	M. Hospital supervisor; Van ____
J - 14.	FIGHT	N. Place Frederick jumped into to escape
S - 15.	RINALDI	O. Friend to Frederick and Catherine
L - 16.	LOVE	P. Place where story takes place
A - 17.	BARKLEY	Q. He helped Frederick and Catherine
I - 18.	HEMORRHAGES	R. Hurt but not killed
Y - 19.	AMERICAN	S. He was going to marry Catherine before Frederick met her.
M - 20.	CAMPEN	T. Was shot by mistake by Italians
K - 21.	SWITZERLAND	U. Catherine thinks he's boring
C - 22.	WISDOM	V. Place where sick & wounded people are treated
X - 23.	HEMINGWAY	W. Hospital where Catherine was transferred
V - 24.	HOSPITAL	X. Author
W 25.	MILAN	Y. Frederick Henry's nationality

MATCHING QUIZ/WORKSHEET 2 - A Farewell To Arms

___ 1. WAR   A. Dear boy, that's not ___. That is cynicism.

___ 2. JAUNDICE   B. A ___ To Arms

___ 3. BROTHERS   C. Feeling of Frederick towards Catherine

___ 4. TRICK   D. He helped Frederick and Catherine

___ 5. RIVER   E. He was going to marry Catherine before Frederick met her.

___ 6. LEG   F. Frederick Henry joined this corps

___ 7. AYMO   G. Where Frederick was wounded

___ 8. RINALDI   H. Rinaldi said he and Frederick were alike underneath; like ___.

___ 9. AMBULANCE   I. Friend to Frederick and Catherine

___ 10. LIFE   J. I am the ___. I am the ___ of reason.

___ 11. PREGNANT   K. Catherine's condition

___ 12. BARKLEY   L. Place where story takes place

___ 13. ALPS   M. Frederick's illness from drinking

___ 14. BRAVE   N. I was going to forget the war. I had made a separate ___.

___ 15. SNAKE   O. Place Frederick jumped into to escape

___ 16. GAGE   P. Catherine's last name

___ 17. LOVE   Q. Frederick played billiards with him

___ 18. MILAN   R. A ___ person dies two thousand deaths but never mentions it

___ 19. PEACE   S. Hospital where Catherine was transferred

___ 20. ITALY   T. Narrator: Frederick _____

___ 21. FAREWELL   U. Name of the mountain range

___ 22. HENRY   V. Was shot by mistake by Italians

___ 23. BARMAN   W. World ___ I

___ 24. GREFFI   X. I'm not a bit afraid. It's just a dirty

___ 25. WISDOM   Y. But ___ isn't hard to manage when you've nothing to lose.

KEY: MATCHING QUIZ/WORKSHEET 2 - A Farewell To Arms

W 1. WAR   A. Dear boy, that's not ___. That is cynicism.
M 2. JAUNDICE   B. A ___ To Arms
H 3. BROTHERS   C. Feeling of Frederick towards Catherine
X 4. TRICK   D. He helped Frederick and Catherine
O 5. RIVER   E. He was going to marry Catherine before Frederick met her.
G 6. LEG   F. Frederick Henry joined this corps
V 7. AYMO   G. Where Frederick was wounded
E 8. RINALDI   H. Rinaldi said he and Frederick were alike underneath; like ___.
F 9. AMBULANCE   I. Friend to Frederick and Catherine
Y 10. LIFE   J. I am the ___. I am the ___ of reason.
K 11. PREGNANT   K. Catherine's condition
P 12. BARKLEY   L. Place where story takes place
U 13. ALPS   M. Frederick's illness from drinking
R 14. BRAVE   N. I was going to forget the war. I had made a separate ___.
J 15. SNAKE   O. Place Frederick jumped into to escape
I 16. GAGE   P. Catherine's last name
C 17. LOVE   Q. Frederick played billiards with him
S 18. MILAN   R. A ___ person dies two thousand deaths but never mentions it
N 19. PEACE   S. Hospital where Catherine was transferred
L 20. ITALY   T. Narrator: Frederick _____
B 21. FAREWELL   U. Name of the mountain range
T 22. HENRY   V. Was shot by mistake by Italians
D 23. BARMAN   W. World ___ I
Q 24. GREFFI   X. I'm not a bit afraid. It's just a dirty
A 25. WISDOM   Y. But ___ isn't hard to manage when you've nothing to lose.

143

JUGGLE LETTER REVIEW GAME CLUE SHEET - A Farewell To Arms

1. SPAL = 1. _____
   Name of the mountain range

2. YALTI = 2. _____
   Place where story takes place

3. EHRRSTBO = 3. _____
   Rinaldi said he and Frederick were alike underneath; like ___.

4. ANDJEIUC = 4. _____
   Frederick's illness from drinking

5. GEAG = 5. _____
   Friend to Frederick and Catherine

6. BEER = 6. _____
   It would help keep the baby small

7. SRPSNAPWEE = 7. _____
   The priest brought Frederick vermouth and ___ in the hospital.

8. UWDONDE = 8. _____
   Hurt but not killed

9. RAW = 9. _____
   World ___ I

10. AIESDLRNZTW =10. _____
    The neutral country

11. LBKRAEY =11. _____
    Catherine's last name

12. GLE =12. _____
    Where Frederick was wounded

13. OLEOLNB =13. _____
    He left Frederick and Piani at the farmhouse

14. ADIRLIN =14. _____
    He was going to marry Catherine before Frederick met her.

15. IHSALTOP =15. _____
    Place where sick & wounded people are treated

16. HGESARRMEHO =16. _____
Catherine died having ___ after the operation

17. OAYM =17. _____
Was shot by mistake by Italians

18. CEPEA =18. _____
I was going to forget the war. I had made a separate ___.

19. ALREWFLE =19. _____
A ___ To Arms

20. RDOSER =20. _____
They must be obeyed

21. SRUNE =21. _____
Catherine's profession

22. NGEAR =22. _____
___ was washed away in the river along with any obligation.

23. NRAI =23. _____
Catherine is afraid of it

24. KNASE =24. _____
I am the ___. I am the ___ of reason.

25. SIODWM =25. _____
Dear boy, that's not ___. That is cynicism.

26. IRFGFE =26. _____
Frederick played billiards with him

27. ELVO =27. _____
Feeling of Frederick towards Catherine

28. NLIAM =28. _____
Hospital where Catherine was transferred

29. ORETTE =29. _____
Catherine thinks he's boring

30. BABY =30. _____
It was born dead

31. NTGNRPAE =31. _____
Catherine's condition

32. TBOA =32. _____
The barman gives Frederick & Catherine a ___ and food

33. RABNAM =33. _____
He helped Frederick and Catherine

34. ITLGH =34. _____
___ For Me; horse they bet on

35. EITPSR =35. _____
Rinaldi teases him, but Frederick shows some respect.

36. RRVIE =36. _____
Place Frederick jumped into to escape

37. AGEWIMYNH =37. _____
Author

38. NLCMUEBAA =38. _____
Frederick Henry joined this corps

39. ADMEL =39. _____
Award

40. ILEF =40. _____
But ___ isn't hard to manage when you've nothing to lose.

41. MARS =41. _____
A Farewell to ___

42. YAOHNTN =42. _____
Catherine gave Frederick a St. ___ medal.

43. ANMPCE =43. _____
Hospital supervisor; Van ____

44. EBVAR =44. _____
A ___ person dies two thousand deaths but never mentions it

45. ETALNIVNI =45. _____
A true Hemingway man; fixed Frederick's knee

46. THGIF =46. _____
In war, one side ____s the other

146

KEY: JUGGLE LETTER REVIEW GAME CLUE SHEET - A Farewell To Arms

1. SPAL = 1. ALPS
   Name of the mountain range

2. YALTI = 2. ITALY
   Place where story takes place

3. EHRRSTBO = 3. BROTHERS
   Rinaldi said he and Frederick were alike underneath; like ___.

4. ANDJEIUC = 4. JAUNDICE
   Frederick's illness from drinking

5. GEAG = 5. GAGE
   Friend to Frederick and Catherine

6. BEER = 6. BEER
   It would help keep the baby small

7. SRPSNAPWEE = 7. NEWSPAPERS
   The priest brought Frederick vermouth and ___ in the hospital.

8. UWDONDE = 8. WOUNDED
   Hurt but not killed

9. RAW = 9. WAR
   World ___ I

10. AIESDLRNZTW =10. SWITZERLAND
    The neutral country

11. LBKRAEY =11. BARKLEY
    Catherine's last name

12. GLE =12. LEG
    Where Frederick was wounded

13. OLEOLNB =13. BONELLO
    He left Frederick and Piani at the farmhouse

14. ADIRLIN =14. RINALDI
    He was going to marry Catherine before Frederick met her.

15. IHSALTOP =15. HOSPITAL
    Place where sick & wounded people are treated

16. HGESARRMEHO =16. HEMORRHAGES
Catherine died having ___ after the operation

17. OAYM =17. AYMO
Was shot by mistake by Italians

18. CEPEA =18. PEACE
I was going to forget the war. I had made a separate ___.

19. ALREWFLE =19. FAREWELL
A ___ To Arms

20. RDOSER =20. ORDERS
They must be obeyed

21. SRUNE =21. NURSE
Catherine's profession

22. NGEAR =22. ANGER
___ was washed away in the river along with any obligation.

23. NRAI =23. RAIN
Catherine is afraid of it

24. KNASE =24. SNAKE
I am the ___. I am the ___ of reason.

25. SIODWM =25. WISDOM
Dear boy, that's not ___. That is cynicism.

26. IRFGFE =26. GREFFI
Frederick played billiards with him

27. ELVO =27. LOVE
Feeling of Frederick towards Catherine

28. NLIAM =28. MILAN
Hospital where Catherine was transferred

29. ORETTE =29. ETTORE
Catherine thinks he's boring

30. BABY =30. BABY
It was born dead

31. NTGNRPAE =31. PREGNANT
Catherine's condition

32. TBOA =32. BOAT
The barman gives Frederick & Catherine a ___ and food

33. RABNAM =33. BARMAN
He helped Frederick and Catherine

34. ITLGH =34. LIGHT
___ For Me; horse they bet on

35. EITPSR =35. PRIEST
Rinaldi teases him, but Frederick shows some respect.

36. RRVIE =36. RIVER
Place Frederick jumped into to escape

37. AGEWIMYNH =37. HEMINGWAY
Author

38. NLCMUEBAA =38. AMBULANCE
Frederick Henry joined this corps

39. ADMEL =39. MEDAL
Award

40. ILEF =40. LIFE
But ___ isn't hard to manage when you've nothing to lose.

41. MARS =41. ARMS
A Farewell to ___

42. YAOHNTN =42. ANTHONY
Catherine gave Frederick a St. ___ medal.

43. ANMPCE =43. CAMPEN
Hospital supervisor; Van ____

44. EBVAR =44. BRAVE
A ___ person dies two thousand deaths but never mentions it

45. ETALNIVNI =45. VALENTINI
A true Hemingway man; fixed Frederick's knee

46. THGIF =46. FIGHT
In war, one side ____s the other

149

VOCABULARY RESOURCE MATERIALS

A Farewell To Arms Vocabulary Word Search 2

```
T R A J E C T O R Y E R H S O C N A C H
R T R T R G G V O C X H W E B I U N T B
N O E W X I W W B A A O F T S T I A N W
H R L F S O D X S L R R A T A S R U F
F R O N T F Y G C L T U A L A T A C N B
X E H Y R F L J E A E C G U C I N H C G
S N C L A E N B N F D K M G L O C I H J
R T D S I N I W E W E S E A E N E S A M
O X I U N S A R R V P A N O S M D T P F
T E S O E I G E A X Y C T C X Y D V E W
A T M U D V N C S M L K S P T T N A R V
T A A T G E U R N S N W T K D C Q G O X
I M L P A A L A E S O Z Y X O B C U N T
G I C M T U C C T R R H E R A Y E E X
A T H E I S T S E I T I L A M R O F D K
H I S T C O U G O N A S R I E E E N E V
O G D N R G I L A C M T O T R M R S T L
S E W O B M A F X D I N T Q S O U Y A M
T L J C E I N S F L S A M Z H R T G L X
I L K N D I L N L Y B O L Q E S C G E Y
L Q T R H T P E V G K P L I D E N O W Y
E P O R T E R D E V O U T E S S U R T K
W C M L G Y Y C Y N I C I S M T P G J G
I N T E R N R U P T U R E L Z N S P Y G
```

AGITATORS	DISMAL	INTERN	SCARCE
ANARCHIST	DORMER	LEGITIMATE	SECTOR
ARTILLERY	ELATED	MATRONLY	SHEDS
ATHEISTS	EMERY	NUISANCE	SOCIALISTS
BATTERY	EVACUATES	OBSCENE	SOLEMN
BELLOWS	EXALTED	OBSTACLES	STRAINED
BILE	FALLACY	OFFENSIVE	TAUT
CAMIONS	FORMALITIES	PORTER	TORRENT
CHOLERA	FRAGMENTS	PRY	TRAJECTORY
CITATION	FRONT	PUNCTURE	TRUSS
COAGULATES	GROGGY	REGIMENT	UNCHAPERONED
CONTEMPTUOUSLY	GUSTS	REMORSE	UNGAINLY
CORDIAL	GYPS	RIDGE	VAGUE
CYNICISM	HOSTILE	RUCKSACK	
DEVOUT	INFANTRY	RUPTURE	

A Farewell To Arms Vocabulary Word Search 2 Answer Key

```
T R A J E C T O R Y E     S   O C   N A
  T   R         O C   X   W E B   I U N
  O   E       I   B A   O F T   S I   A
  R   L   S   O   S L   R R A   T T   R
F R O N T   F Y G C L   T E L   A I   C U
  E   H   T R   L E A   E G U   T O   H N
S N   C   R A   E N F   D M G   L N   A C
  T   D   A I   N   E   E E A   E     P H
R O   I   S N   S   V   D S O   S     E A
  T   S   O E   I G E   Y A C         R P
A A   M   U D   V N C   L K         D O E
T     A   T     E R     N   S     C Y N R
T I   L   P     A A E S O   Y   E A U E O
I G   E   M     U C R R R   L   R M E D N
A T   I   S     S E I T I   A   O E   E E
H H   S   T     O G N A R   M   E R   T D
O I     R O     U A N C I   E   S U   A  
S G     B M     G L   M T   R   O T   L  
T E     C E     I F   I N   S   R G   E  
I L     N D     L L   S A   H   S C    
L       R       E P   B O   L   E N    
E       T P     L E   O L   I   D O    
  P O R T E R D E V O U T E S S   U R T
    Y Y C Y N I C I S M     N   P G    
I N T E R N R U P T U R E       S P Y G
```

AGITATORS   DISMAL   INTERN   SCARCE

ANARCHIST   DORMER   LEGITIMATE   SECTOR

ARTILLERY   ELATED   MATRONLY   SHEDS

ATHEISTS   EMERY   NUISANCE   SOCIALISTS

BATTERY   EVACUATES   OBSCENE   SOLEMN

BELLOWS   EXALTED   OBSTACLES   STRAINED

BILE   FALLACY   OFFENSIVE   TAUT

CAMIONS   FORMALITIES   PORTER   TORRENT

CHOLERA   FRAGMENTS   PRY   TRAJECTORY

CITATION   FRONT   PUNCTURE   TRUSS

COAGULATES   GROGGY   REGIMENT   UNCHAPERONED

CONTEMPTUOUSLY   GUSTS   REMORSE   UNGAINLY

CORDIAL   GYPS   RIDGE   VAGUE

CYNICISM   HOSTILE   RUCKSACK

DEVOUT   INFANTRY   RUPTURE

A Farewell To Arms Vocabulary Crossword

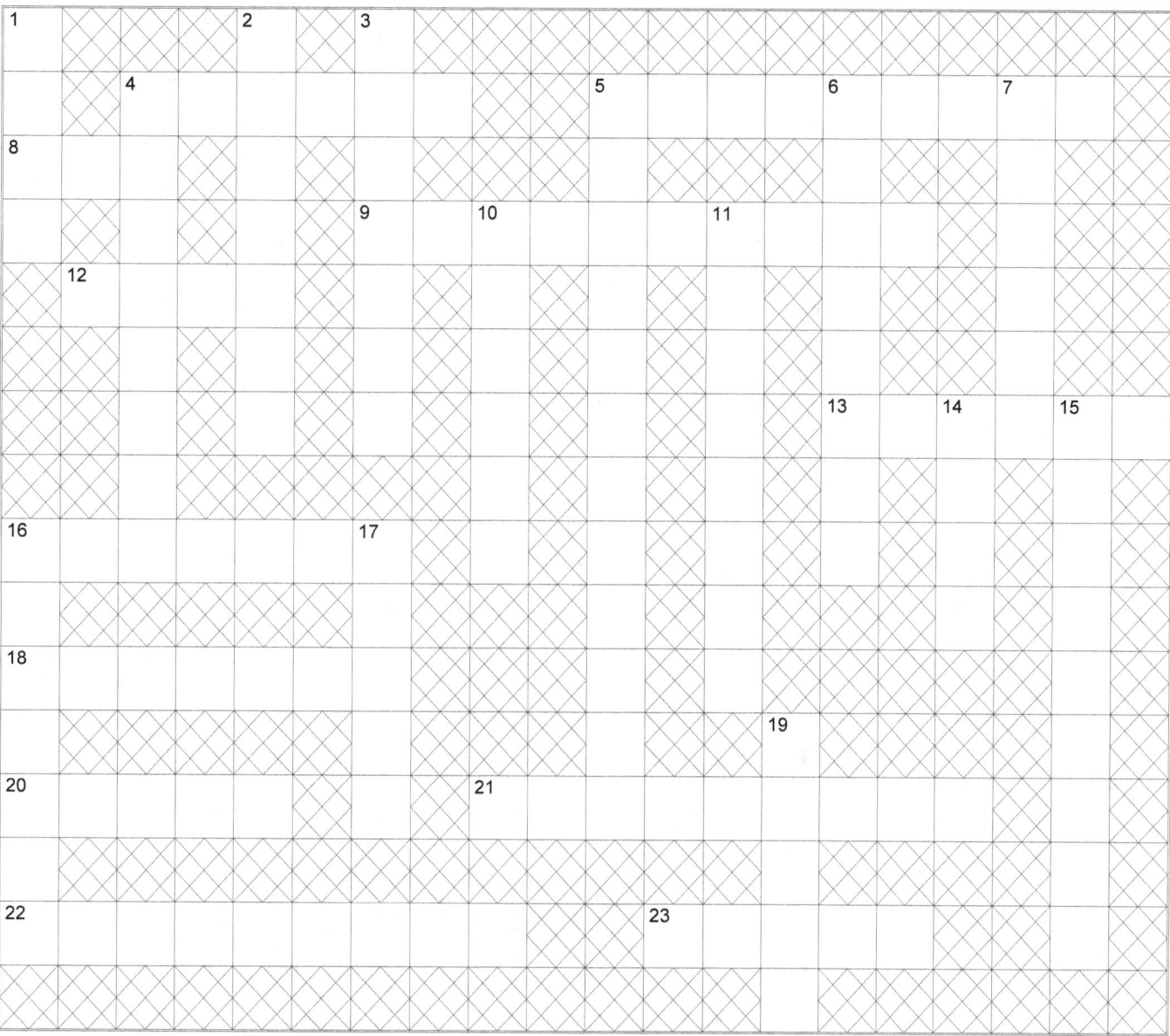

Across
4. Traditional Swiss wooden cottage
5. One who thinks government should be abandoned
8. Force apart or open with a lever
9. Legal; lawful
12. Fluid produced in the liver
13. Put in prison
16. Buses or trucks
18. Morally offensive
20. Sandpaper
21. Having a very high opinion of oneself
22. Protesters; troublemakers
23. Not clear in meaning

Down
1. Cheats out of money
2. Unit of guns or other weapons
3. Shouts in a loud, deep voice
4. Negative sarcasm or mockery
5. Connection; fitting together
6. Official document of praise
7. In short or limited supply
10. Weak or dizzy; not fully alert
11. Like a mature woman with sensible qualities
14. Tense; tight
15. Held back; kept from doing
16. A disease of the intestines caused by bacteria
17. Causes water to flow or drop off
19. Long, narrow hilltop

A Farewell To Arms Vocabulary Crossword Answer Key

	1 G		2 B		3 B							
	Y		4 C	H	A	L	E	T		5 A	N	A	R	6 C	H	7 I	S	T
	8 P	R	Y		T			L		R				I			C	
	S		N		T		9 L	E	10 G	I	T	11 I	M	A	T	E	A	
		12 B	I	L	E		O		R		I		A		A		R	
			C		R		W		O		C		T		T	13 I	14 N	15 T	E	R	N
			I		Y		S		G		U		R		O		O		A		E
			S						G		L		O		O		A		E	
16 C	A	M	I	O	N	S		17 S		Y		A		N		N		U		F
H								H				T		L				T		R
18 O	B	S	C	E	N	E						I		Y						A
L						D						O				19 R				I
20 E	M	E	R	Y				21 C	O	N	C	E	I	T	E	D				N
R																D				E
22 A	G	I	T	A	T	O	R	S		23 V	A	G	U	E						D
										E										

Across
4. Traditional Swiss wooden cottage
5. One who thinks government should be abandoned
8. Force apart or open with a lever
9. Legal; lawful
12. Fluid produced in the liver
13. Put in prison
16. Buses or trucks
18. Morally offensive
20. Sandpaper
21. Having a very high opinion of oneself
22. Protesters; troublemakers
23. Not clear in meaning

Down
1. Cheats out of money
2. Unit of guns or other weapons
3. Shouts in a loud, deep voice
4. Negative sarcasm or mockery
5. Connection; fitting together
6. Official document of praise
7. In short or limited supply
10. Weak or dizzy; not fully alert
11. Like a mature woman with sensible qualities
14. Tense; tight
15. Held back; kept from doing
16. A disease of the intestines caused by bacteria
17. Causes water to flow or drop off
19. Long, narrow hilltop

VOCABULARY MATCHING WORKSHEET 1 - A Farewell To Arms

___ 1. ANARCHIST   A. Buses or trucks
___ 2. NUISANCE   B. Started
___ 3. INVIGORATING   C. Traditional Swiss wooden cottage
___ 4. CHALET   D. Being weak and likely to break or crack
___ 5. EVACUATES   E. Full of tension; nervous
___ 6. BRITTLENESS   F. Clumsy; not graceful
___ 7. IMPARTIALLY   G. Filling with energy
___ 8. UNGAINLY   H. One who is hired to carry baggage
___ 9. CONCEITED   I. In a disapproving way
___10. TOURNIQUET   J. Tight band used to stop bleeding
___11. DEVOUT   K. Lasting for a long time
___12. PROTRACTED   L. A disease of the intestines caused by bacteria
___13. CHOLERA   M. Leaves a dangerous place
___14. PORTER   N. Soldiers who fight on foot
___15. CYNICISM   O. Sudden, violent bursts of wind
___16. COMMENCED   P. Cheats out of money
___17. INFANTRY   Q. Having a very high opinion of oneself
___18. RIDGE   R. Very religious
___19. GUSTS   S. Negative sarcasm or mockery
___20. FORMALITIES   T. Strong feeling of guilt or sorrow
___21. CAMIONS   U. Long, narrow hilltop
___22. GYPS   V. One who thinks government should be abandoned
___23. REMORSE   W. Annoyance; irritation
___24. STRAINED   X. Official procedures that must be followed
___25. CONTEMPTUOUSLY   Y. Fairly

KEY: VOCABULARY MATCHING WORKSHEET 1 - A Farewell To Arms

V - 1. ANARCHIST	A. Buses or trucks
W - 2. NUISANCE	B. Started
G - 3. INVIGORATING	C. Traditional Swiss wooden cottage
C - 4. CHALET	D. Being weak and likely to break or crack
M - 5. EVACUATES	E. Full of tension; nervous
D - 6. BRITTLENESS	F. Clumsy; not graceful
Y - 7. IMPARTIALLY	G. Filling with energy
F - 8. UNGAINLY	H. One who is hired to carry baggage
Q - 9. CONCEITED	I. In a disapproving way
J - 10. TOURNIQUET	J. Tight band used to stop bleeding
R - 11. DEVOUT	K. Lasting for a long time
K - 12. PROTRACTED	L. A disease of the intestines caused by bacteria
L - 13. CHOLERA	M. Leaves a dangerous place
H - 14. PORTER	N. Soldiers who fight on foot
S - 15. CYNICISM	O. Sudden, violent bursts of wind
B - 16. COMMENCED	P. Cheats out of money
N - 17. INFANTRY	Q. Having a very high opinion of oneself
U - 18. RIDGE	R. Very religious
O - 19. GUSTS	S. Negative sarcasm or mockery
X - 20. FORMALITIES	T. Strong feeling of guilt or sorrow
A - 21. CAMIONS	U. Long, narrow hilltop
P - 22. GYPS	V. One who thinks government should be abandoned
T - 23. REMORSE	W. Annoyance; irritation
E - 24. STRAINED	X. Official procedures that must be followed
I - 25. CONTEMPTUOUSLY	Y. Fairly

VOCABULARY MATCHING WORKSHEET 2 - A Farewell To Arms

___ 1. FALLACY   A. People who believe in control by the people

___ 2. GYPS   B. A disease of the intestines caused by bacteria

___ 3. CORDIAL   C. A grouping of military troops

___ 4. DOMINEERING   D. Like a mature woman with sensible qualities

___ 5. MATRONLY   E. Pleasant; friendly

___ 6. HEMORRHAGE   F. Official document of praise

___ 7. IMPARTIALLY   G. Bleeding; a loss of blood

___ 8. ATHEISTS   H. Route; path

___ 9. CONCEITED   I. Full of tension; nervous

___ 10. SOLEMN   J. People who do not believe in God

___ 11. TRAJECTORY   K. Connection; fitting together

___ 12. CHOLERA   L. Thickens; clots; sticks together

___ 13. STRAINED   M. Praiseworthy

___ 14. BELLOWS   N. Belief that is actually incorrect

___ 15. BRITTLENESS   O. Bossy or controlling

___ 16. ARTICULATION   P. Serious; humorless

___ 17. UNGAINLY   Q. Tense; tight

___ 18. TAUT   R. Being weak and likely to break or crack

___ 19. SOCIALISTS   S. Clumsy; not graceful

___ 20. LEGITIMATE   T. Legal; lawful

___ 21. SCRUTINIZING   U. Having a very high opinion of oneself

___ 22. EXALTED   V. Cheats out of money

___ 23. REGIMENT   W. Fairly

___ 24. CITATION   X. Examining carefully

___ 25. COAGULATES   Y. Shouts in a loud, deep voice

KEY: VOCABULARY MATCHING WORKSHEET 2 - A Farewell To Arms

N - 1. FALLACY		A. People who believe in control by the people
V - 2. GYPS		B. A disease of the intestines caused by bacteria
E - 3. CORDIAL		C. A grouping of military troops
O - 4. DOMINEERING		D. Like a mature woman with sensible qualities
D - 5. MATRONLY		E. Pleasant; friendly
G - 6. HEMORRHAGE		F. Official document of praise
W - 7. IMPARTIALLY		G. Bleeding; a loss of blood
J - 8. ATHEISTS		H. Route; path
U - 9. CONCEITED		I. Full of tension; nervous
P - 10. SOLEMN		J. People who do not believe in God
H - 11. TRAJECTORY		K. Connection; fitting together
B - 12. CHOLERA		L. Thickens; clots; sticks together
I - 13. STRAINED		M. Praiseworthy
Y - 14. BELLOWS		N. Belief that is actually incorrect
R - 15. BRITTLENESS		O. Bossy or controlling
K - 16. ARTICULATION		P. Serious; humorless
S - 17. UNGAINLY		Q. Tense; tight
Q - 18. TAUT		R. Being weak and likely to break or crack
A - 19. SOCIALISTS		S. Clumsy; not graceful
T - 20. LEGITIMATE		T. Legal; lawful
X - 21. SCRUTINIZING		U. Having a very high opinion of oneself
M - 22. EXALTED		V. Cheats out of money
C - 23. REGIMENT		W. Fairly
F - 24. CITATION		X. Examining carefully
L - 25. COAGULATES		Y. Shouts in a loud, deep voice

VOCABULARY JUGGLE LETTER REVIEW GAME CLUE SHEET 1 - A Farewell To Arms

1. ORDACIL = 1. _____
   Pleasant; friendly

2. RPY = 2. _____
   Force apart or open with a lever

3. KUASRCKC = 3. _____
   Backpack

4. AGTILETEIM = 4. _____
   Legal; lawful

5. XLETADE = 5. _____
   Praiseworthy

6. NGRNVOIIITAG = 6. _____
   Filling with energy

7. LSEOMN = 7. _____
   Serious; humorless

8. LARTTINUIAOC = 8. _____
   Connection; fitting together

9. MNGEIRET = 9. _____
   A grouping of military troops

10. ASAGITRTO =10. _____
    Protesters; troublemakers

11. YTARMLON =11. _____
    Like a mature woman with sensible qualities

12. MNOELYCUTOUSPT =12. _____
    In a disapproving way

13. SROMFAETIIL =13. _____
    Official procedures that must be followed

14. DELAET =14. _____
    Happy and excited

15. ERNTNI =15. _____
    Put in prison

16. INEDECCOT   =16. _____
                        Having a very high opinion of oneself

17. ETBLTRNESSI   =17. _____
                        Being weak and likely to break or crack

18. RPERTUU   =18. _____
                        A tear in tissue in the body; a hernia

19. CPTTDEARRO   =19. _____
                        Lasting for a long time

20. JOTRLIEPEC   =20. _____
                        Bullet; shell

21. EEHORAGMHR   =21. _____
                        Bleeding; a loss of blood

22. ERBTAYT   =22. _____
                        Unit of guns or other weapons

23. ACOSMNI   =23. _____
                        Buses or trucks

24. HSDSE   =24. _____
                        Causes water to flow or drop off

25. TOILSSSICA   =25. _____
                        People who believe in control by the people

26. DBAQSULEB   =26. _____
                        Argued

27. ATIDNERS   =27. _____
                        Full of tension; nervous

28. LIMDAS   =28. _____
                        Gloomy; depressing

29. CPADOEUENRNH   =29. _____
                        Not accompanied by a supervisor

30. SAVAETCEU   =30. _____
                        Leaves a dangerous place

31. UTTA   =31. _____
                        Tense; tight

32. SLELBOW =32. _____
Shouts in a loud, deep voice

33. HTAIETSS =33. _____
People who do not believe in God

34. UOVEDT =34. _____
Very religious

35. SUTRS =35. _____
Medical device used to support a hernia

36. IEBL =36. _____
Fluid produced in the liver

KEY: VOCABULARY JUGGLE LETTER REVIEW GAME CLUE SHEET 1 - A Farewell To Arms

1. ORDACIL = 1. CORDIAL
Pleasant; friendly

2. RPY = 2. PRY
Force apart or open with a lever

3. KUASRCKC = 3. RUCKSACK
Backpack

4. AGTILETEIM = 4. LEGITIMATE
Legal; lawful

5. XLETADE = 5. EXALTED
Praiseworthy

6. NGRNVOIIITAG = 6. INVIGORATING
Filling with energy

7. LSEOMN = 7. SOLEMN
Serious; humorless

8. LARTTINUIAOC = 8. ARTICULATION
Connection; fitting together

9. MNGEIRET = 9. REGIMENT
A grouping of military troops

10. ASAGITRTO = 10. AGITATORS
Protesters; troublemakers

11. YTARMLON = 11. MATRONLY
Like a mature woman with sensible qualities

12. MNOELYCUTOUSPT = 12. CONTEMPTUOUSLY
In a disapproving way

13. SROMFAETIIL = 13. FORMALITIES
Official procedures that must be followed

14. DELAET = 14. ELATED
Happy and excited

15. ERNTNI = 15. INTERN
Put in prison

16. INEDECCOT =16. CONCEITED
Having a very high opinion of oneself

17. ETBLTRNESSI =17. BRITTLENESS
Being weak and likely to break or crack

18. RPERTUU =18. RUPTURE
A tear in tissue in the body; a hernia

19. CPTTDEARRO =19. PROTRACTED
Lasting for a long time

20. JOTRLIEPEC =20. PROJECTILE
Bullet; shell

21. EEHORAGMHR =21. HEMORRHAGE
Bleeding; a loss of blood

22. ERBTAYT =22. BATTERY
Unit of guns or other weapons

23. ACOSMNI =23. CAMIONS
Buses or trucks

24. HSDSE =24. SHEDS
Causes water to flow or drop off

25. TOILSSSICA =25. SOCIALISTS
People who believe in control by the people

26. DBAQSULEB =26. SQUABBLED
Argued

27. ATIDNERS =27. STRAINED
Full of tension; nervous

28. LIMDAS =28. DISMAL
Gloomy; depressing

29. CPADOEUENRNH =29. UNCHAPERONED
Not accompanied by a supervisor

30. SAVAETCEU =30. EVACUATES
Leaves a dangerous place

31. UTTA =31. TAUT
Tense; tight

32. SLELBOW =32 BELLOWS

Shouts in a loud, deep voice

33. HTAIETSS =33. ATHEISTS

People who do not believe in God

34. UOVEDT =34. DEVOUT

Very religious

35. SUTRS =35. TRUSS

Medical device used to support a hernia

36. IEBL =36. BILE

Fluid produced in the liver

VOCABULARY JUGGLE LETTER REVIEW GAME CLUE SHEET 2 - A Farewell To Arms

1. CSTREO = 1. _____
   Zone; division

2. AXIILETROHAN = 2. _____
   Happiness and excitement

3. YGOGGR = 3. _____
   Weak or dizzy; not fully alert

4. JATREROTYC = 4. _____
   Route; path

5. YEREM = 5. _____
   Sandpaper

6. SIYCMCIN = 6. _____
   Negative sarcasm or mockery

7. TAITOINC = 7. _____
   Official document of praise

8. EALCHT = 8. _____
   Traditional Swiss wooden cottage

9. ECSRCA = 9. _____
   In short or limited supply

10. LYCLFAA =10. _____
    Belief that is actually incorrect

11. ERTNTRO =11. _____
    Fast, powerful flood of water

12. LPIIYMRATAL =12. _____
    Fairly

13. FOEIVNESF =13. _____
    An attack or assault

14. TSMFGENRA =14. _____
    Small pieces of something shattered

15. GLANNYIU =15. _____
    Clumsy; not graceful

16. TRUENTOUQI =16. _____
Tight band used to stop bleeding

17. SDGSREIN =17. _____
Bandages & things pertaining to treating wounds

18. TUCUNERP =18. _____
Reduce someone's confidence

19. ORDMER =19. _____
Window built at right angles to the roof

20. PERTRO =20. _____
One who is hired to carry baggage

21. UELSOTCGAA =21. _____
Thickens; clots; sticks together

22. NEOSBCE =22. _____
Morally offensive

23. EOTLSHI =23. _____
Unfriendly; showing hatred toward another

24. TORFN =24. _____
The leading position in a war

25. IGRDE =25. _____
Long, narrow hilltop

26. LYLETRARI =26. _____
Large guns and cannons

27. IITGNRCSIZNU =27. _____
Examining carefully

28. NSHIRAATC =28. _____
One who thinks government should be abandoned

29. EVAUG =29. _____
Not clear in meaning

30. PYSG =30. _____
Cheats out of money

31. AHRLEOC =31. _____
A disease of the intestines caused by bacteria

32. CNENISUA =32. _____
　　　　　　　　　Annoyance; irritation

33. NTEMESTNI =33. _____
　　　　　　　　　Thoughts based on feelings

34. SGTSU =34. _____
　　　　　　　　　Sudden, violent bursts of wind

35. YNANRFTI =35. _____
　　　　　　　　　Soldiers who fight on foot

36. EIRIONMGEND =36. _____
　　　　　　　　　Bossy or controlling

KEY: VOCABULARY JUGGLE LETTER REVIEW GAME CLUE SHEET 2 - A Farewell To Arms

1. CSTREO = 1. SECTOR
   Zone; division

2. AXIILETROHAN = 2. EXHILARATION
   Happiness and excitement

3. YGOGGR = 3. GROGGY
   Weak or dizzy; not fully alert

4. JATREROTYC = 4. TRAJECTORY
   Route; path

5. YEREM = 5. EMERY
   Sandpaper

6. SIYCMCIN = 6. CYNICISM
   Negative sarcasm or mockery

7. TAITOINC = 7. CITATION
   Official document of praise

8. EALCHT = 8. CHALET
   Traditional Swiss wooden cottage

9. ECSRCA = 9. SCARCE
   In short or limited supply

10. LYCLFAA = 10. FALLACY
    Belief that is actually incorrect

11. ERTNTRO = 11. TORRENT
    Fast, powerful flood of water

12. LPIIYMRATAL = 12. IMPARTIALLY
    Fairly

13. FOEIVNESF = 13. OFFENSIVE
    An attack or assault

14. TSMFGENRA = 14. FRAGMENTS
    Small pieces of something shattered

15. GLANNYIU = 15. UNGAINLY
    Clumsy; not graceful

16. TRUENTOUQI =16. TOURNIQUET
Tight band used to stop bleeding

17. SDGSREIN =17. DRESSING
Bandages & things pertaining to treating wounds

18. TUCUNERP =18. PUNCTURE
Reduce someone's confidence

19. ORDMER =19. DORMER
Window built at right angles to the roof

20. PERTRO =20. PORTER
One who is hired to carry baggage

21. UELSOTCGAA =21. COAGULATES
Thickens; clots; sticks together

22. NEOSBCE =22. OBSCENE
Morally offensive

23. EOTLSHI =23. HOSTILE
Unfriendly; showing hatred toward another

24. TORFN =24. FRONT
The leading position in a war

25. IGRDE =25. RIDGE
Long, narrow hilltop

26. LYLETRARI =26. ARTILLERY
Large guns and cannons

27. IITGNRCSIZNU =27. SCRUTINIZING
Examining carefully

28. NSHIRAATC =28. ANARCHIST
One who thinks government should be abandoned

29. EVAUG =29. VAGUE
Not clear in meaning

30. PYSG =30. GYPS
Cheats out of money

31. AHRLEOC =31. CHOLERA
A disease of the intestines caused by bacteria

32. CNENISUA =32. NUISANCE
Annoyance; irritation

33. NTEMESTNI =33. SENTIMENT
Thoughts based on feelings

34. SGTSU =34. GUSTS
Sudden, violent bursts of wind

35. YNANRFTI =35. INFANTRY
Soldiers who fight on foot

36. EIRIONMGEND =36. DOMINEERING
Bossy or controlling

www.ingramcontent.com/pod-product-compliance
Lightning Source LLC
Chambersburg PA
CBHW051407070526
44584CB00023B/3329